DAYS OF A RUSSIAN NOBLEWOMAN

~~~ DAYS OF A ~~~
RUSSIAN NOBLEWOMAN
~~~~~~~~~~~~~~~~~~

THE MEMORIES OF
ANNA LABZINA
1758–1821

Translated and Edited by

Gary Marker and Rachel May

NORTHERN ILLINOIS UNIVERSITY PRESS

DeKalb

Published by the Northern Illinois University Press, DeKalb, Illinois   60115

Manufactured in the United States using acid-free paper

Design by Julia Fauci

Library of Congress Cataloging-in-Publication Data

Labzina, Anna Evdokimovna, 1758–1828.

[Vospominaniia. English]

Days of a Russian noblewoman: the memories of Anna Labzina,

1758–1821/edited by Gary Marker and Rachel May.

p. cm.

Contents: Memoir—Diary—Appendices: Variant beginning to memoir.

Freemasons' ceremony.

ISBN 0-87580-277-X (alk. paper)

1. Labzina, Anna Evdokimovna, 1758–1828. 2. Nobility—Russia—Biography.

3. Women—Russia—Biography. 4. Labzin, Aleksandr, 1766–1825.

5. Karamyshev, Aleksandr Matveevich, 1744–1791.

6. Russia—Social life and customs—1533–1917. I. Marker, Gary, 1948–

II. May, Rachel. III. Title.

DK127.5.L3 A3 2001

947'.07'092—dc21

2001030061

Contents

The Memories of Anna Labzina
An Introduction by Gary Marker and Rachel May   vii

The Memories of Anna Labzina

AN INTRODUCTION

Gary Marker and Rachel May

On November 28, 1756, Anna Evdokimovna Yakovleva was born into the family of a middling hereditary provincial nobleman. Her father, Evdokim Yakovlevich Yakovlev, was a retired state counselor[1] and was already sixty-four years old when Anna was born. They lived on the family estate outside of the mining town of Ekaterinburg, in the eastern part of European Russia, about one thousand miles from the capital, St. Petersburg. Anna was only seven years old when her father died, in 1764. Though her mother was forty years younger than her father, she too died when Anna was merely thirteen, leaving Anna and two younger brothers.

In death's grip, Anna's mother arranged for her to be married to the son of a close friend, Alexander Matveevich Karamyshev. It promised to be a good match. Karamyshev, then twenty-eight years old, was both nobly born and impressive in his own right, well educated, well placed socially, and in the early stages of what would become a highly successful career in the College of Mines and in scientific exploration.

This marriage lasted nearly twenty years, until Karamyshev's death in 1791. Over that time the couple lived among the most celebrated figures of Russian letters and society. Their acquaintances included M. M. Kheraskov, the greatest epic poet of the day, Prince Grigorii Potemkin, one of Russia's most eminent statesmen and a favorite of the empress, Catherine the Great, and, for a time, even the empress herself. The Karamyshevs had no children, but their life was rich in other experiences. As a result of Alexander Matveevich's professional career they traveled widely within the vast Russian Empire, from the suburbs of the capital to the Chinese border, from the southern Volga to the Pacific Far East. It was not a happy marriage, however, as Labzina's memoir attests. The couple had little in common: Alexander Matveevich belittled his wife's naive and severe piety, and Anna Evdokimovna could not countenance his atheistic free thinking and fondness for pleasures of the flesh.

Three years after Karamyshev's death in 1794, Anna Evdokimovna married another prominent governmental official and man of letters, Alexander Fedorovich Labzin. Eight years her junior, Labzin reintroduced Anna to the elite of Russian letters during the first quarter of the nineteenth century. The Labzins were also childless, but they raised two wards, one a niece and the other the daughter of a deceased friend. By all accounts theirs was a happy marriage, surviving even the travails of internal exile to far-off Simbirsk in 1822 (the result of Labzin's having insulted several aristocrats who were personally close to the emperor). Alexander Fedorovich died in 1825 while still in exile. After his death Anna moved to Moscow, where she died at the age of seventy on October 3, 1828.

If these external facts were all we knew, Labzina's life could be comfortably consigned to the category of "interesting but not especially memorable." The events she relates do not rise to the sensational level achieved by some other notable women of her day. Labzina avoided outrageous or publicly rebellious behavior, and she never tried to masquerade as a man, as did her notorious contemporary memoirist, Nadezhda Durova, who joined the Russian Imperial Army during the Napoleonic Wars.[2] Nor did Labzina participate in palace intrigue and conspiracy, like another female memoirist of the period, Ekaterina Dashkova.[3] Dashkova's memoirs are full of inside information regarding important events, whereas Labzina sticks mostly to the intimate affairs of her own family. Although an active participant in her second husband's journals, Anna worked mostly behind the scenes and published almost nothing in her own lifetime. She held no office (Dashkova had been President of the Russian Academy, and, for a time, of the Academy of Sciences), wrote no essays or literature, and, except for the three years between 1791 and 1794, spent her entire adult life within the confines of marital domesticity, willingly subordinate to her husband.

In lieu of momentous or sensational events, Labzina's auto-biographical writings give us an extraordinary, indeed unique, glimpse into family life in her time. Though Dashkova, Durova, and Catherine II herself wrote memoirs of their public lives, it is far more rare to find an account of the private life of an educated noble family, especially from a woman's viewpoint.[4] Moreover, Labzina left behind not one but two autobiographical writings: a memoir written in 1810 and a one-of-a-kind diary composed over several months during 1818 and 1819. No one else of her era, male or female, composed both a memoir and a personal diary, and although these two documents describe different times in her life, they offer a unique counterpoint, the possibility of reading and comparing two memory texts written by the same person, in two distinct formats and genres. It is in this sense that we speak of the *memories* of Anna Labzina.

HISTORICAL BACKGROUND: RUSSIA IN 1800

The Russian Empire of Labzina's day (late eighteenth and early nineteenth century) was a sprawling, if sparsely populated, behemoth stretching from the Baltic Sea in the west to the Pacific Ocean in the east. Between those borders lived forty to fifty million people, most of them poor and unfree, and many of them—more than half by some recent estimates—non-Russian.[5] One of the great attractions of Labzina's writing is her ability, in a relatively brief space, to reflect on all of these realities. Born and raised deep in the provinces, she spent much of her first marriage traveling far and wide in European Russia, Siberia, and the Russian Far East. Her memoir sometimes reads like a travelogue, and it is filled with tales of Tatars, Bashkirs, Cossacks, and other non-Russian subjects.

Invariably these peoples are described as alien and mysterious, often dangerous, but susceptible to the pacifying power of the faith and the ministrations of Labzina and her mother. A far-flung and seemingly savage empire was tamed and, in Labzina's rendering, available to the civilizing mission of Russian culture, in the form of faith and charity, and through the particular agency of women.

The power of faith over the empire's fearsomeness extended as well to personal contact with Russia's notorious exile system, whose unfortunate souls had been convicted of serious crimes and sentenced to several years in exile in the farthest reaches of Siberia. Some of the most moving scenes of the memoir involve Labzina's face-to-face encounters with individual exiles, the disfigured and violent Feklist or the disgraced nobleman Nikolai Ozerov for example, whom she comes to know and respect as individuals, even as they, too, come to call her "mother."

Labzina's world was stratified in other ways as well. According to the official census, over 90 percent of the population consisted of peasants, and most of them lived in one or another form of bondage, typically either as a serf (in bondage to a private landlord) or as a state peasant (living on state-owned property). The peasants she discussed—bailiffs, household servants, nannies—were, by and large, serfs. By law, their lords had immense power over them, including control of where they lived, where they worked, and even whom they married. In reality, most peasants lived in remote villages and had only infrequent contact with the landlord, but the household servants whom we see frequently in the memoir fell under the direct authority of their owners, whose decisions they could not legally challenge. For all her charity and compassion, Labzina appears to have accepted these social boundaries without reservations, and she felt deep fulfillment when these social dependents came to see her as "mother."

In spite of her personal pain and worry about money, Labzina lived in relative privilege, even affluence, compared to all but a tiny fraction of Russia's subjects. Surrounded by servants and nannies, she learned of physical labor not out of necessity, but because of choices her mother made in raising her. Although far removed from the seclusion of the Muscovite *terem*,[6] Russian noblewomen of Labzina's day still were expected to remain obedient and submissive to the authority of fathers, husbands, and benefactors. In this regard Labzina was entirely representative of her era and social estate. Although able to own property, including land, noblewomen were almost entirely dependent on marriage for their own and their family's economic security. Forbidden from entering the professions or state service, their well-being required connection to a stable household. It is for this reason that Anna's dying mother arranged for her thirteen-year-old daughter to be married.

By these narrowly material standards Labzina made two good matches during her life. Both Karamyshev and Labzin were reasonably well-to-do and well connected. Karamyshev had especially close connections with important officials, and several of these played important roles in providing for the material security of the Karamyshev household, at least so far as they could. Early in the marriage Labzina's own benefactor was the eminent literary and political figure, M. M. Kheraskov, with whom the couple lived while Karamyshev worked in St. Petersburg. Here Labzina was literally surrounded by what might be termed the sheltered luxury of the wealthy noble household, and she was introduced to numerous luminaries at Kheraskov's soirees. Befriended and counseled by both Kheraskov and his wife Elisaveta Vasil'evna Kheraskova, an author in her own right, Labzina was nevertheless obliged to observe the enforced submissiveness and chatty sociability that was the common lot of society women of the day. Her memoir offers a running commentary on these gilded limitations, which she simultaneously submits to yet confronts.

Overlaying the general ethic of sociability, which demanded female submissiveness and worshipfulness, was Freemasonry—a doctrine that seems to have been fundamental in shaping Labzina's worldview. We do not know whether Karamyshev himself was a Mason, but otherwise Labzina was constantly in the company of leading and committed Freemasons during her entire adult life. Her benefactor, Kheraskov, was one of the most important Masons of his day. Labzin himself was the Grand Master of the Dying Sphinx lodge, so deeply immersed in the spirituality of Freemasonry that one recent scholar has dubbed him Russia's leading mystic. Masonic values surrounded Labzina, and their tone and language permeate her writing, especially the diary. Her concerns for the inner self, for moral purity, obedience, self-knowledge, and emotional awareness were central features of Masonic discourse, especially in the ethereal atmosphere of those who, like Labzin, occupied the highest orders ("the inner circle") of the Masonic movement. Like the Masons, Labzina stressed service to humanity as a fundamentally religious obligation. Charity, prayer, and tending the sick and unfortunate were all derived from the word of God the Father and his commandments, and their exercise served both worldly improvement and the pursuit of grace.

At the other extreme of eighteenth-century sociability stood Karamyshev, whose carnal and libertine way of life corresponded to what was known as "Russian Voltairianism." As a celebration of high living, gambling, drinking, and other pursuits of pleasure, Voltairianism was reviled by self-styled serious intellectuals, who saw it as a frivolous perversion of reason and human potential. Among those most offended by this libertinism were the very Freemasons whom Labzina revered. Little wonder, then, that this marriage proved so painful to her.

WOMEN'S AUTOBIOGRAPHICAL WRITINGS

When she wrote her memoir and diary Labzina had few if any female antecedents in Russian culture. Like Labzina's own writings, which appeared in print only in the twentieth century, most women's autobiographical writings remained in obscurity long after they were written. The only such writing that would have been available to Labzina was that of Nataliia Dolgorukaia, whose 1767 text was published for the first time in 1810. This was the same year that Labzina began to write her memoir, and some of her passages are reminiscent of Dolgorukaia's. Otherwise, there was not a single Russian woman's memoir in print when Labzina sat down to write. Catherine the Great's notorious memoir, apparently written in the 1770s, was not published until 1858. N. M. Stroganova's diary of her travels to western Europe in 1781 first came out in 1914. V. I. Bakunina wrote in the 1790s, but her work saw print only in the 1880s. Similarly, Dashkova penned her memoir in 1805, but it was not published until 1840, and then only in English. And finally, Durova's memoir of life in the cavalry during the Napoleonic Wars appeared in print only in 1836. Male memoir writing had become more widespread, but here too there was generally a time lag before a work was published, and the works rarely appeared during the author's own lifetime. According to the Russian scholar A. G. Tartakovskii, only about a dozen had come into print by 1810. Thus, while the act of memoir writing had become a relatively familiar activity among literary Russians, few memoirs were publicly available.

Diary writing was even rarer, and Tartakovskii has identified only two Russian diaries that were in print when Labzina began recording hers. These were the European travel log of the aristocrat N. A. Demidov (published in 1786) and the court diary of S. A. Poroshin, the tutor of the future Paul I (published in 1810). Neither of these, moreover, bears any resemblance to the highly affective and personal observations that Labzina committed to paper.[7]

So far as we know, Labzina wrote her own life with no immediate autobiographical models or canons to guide her. Where then did she draw her inspiration? Where, indeed, did she come up with the idea to write a memoir, or the conviction that autobiography, even written "for the drawer," was an appropriate activity for an apparently domestic and nominally unrebellious woman? To address this question we must engage in a certain amount of speculation, since Labzina's own words provide few direct hints.

Some scholars, struck by the pervasively religious and penitential tone of the texts, have seen affinities with religious biographical and autobiographical traditions. In the introduction to the 1996 edition of Labzina's memoir, for example, V. M. Bokova compares it, with some justice, to the tradition of Russian saints' lives and to the autohagiography of Archpriest

Avvakum.[8] A charismatic priest who led the seventeenth-century rebellion of Old Believers against the official Orthodox church, and who suffered and died for his rebellion, Avvakum wrote a dramatic account of his trials that alternates between folksy narration of the details of his life and weighty, impassioned invocations of his religious beliefs.[9] Like Labzina, Avvakum portrayed himself as a martyr to faith against a more powerful worldly force. The similarities stop there, however. Avvakum was writing a public memoir intended to influence policy and establish his own claim to sainthood, whereas Labzina set out merely to "describe my life, as much as I remember it." She never completed the text and made no effort to publish it, or even to let others know of its existence. Thus, her ideal audience, if she had one, was far more private than Avvakum's. Since Avvakum's autobiography circulated only in hand-copied tracts and was little known among educated society of her day, it is highly unlikely that Labzina was familiar with it.

A more plausible source of inspiration came from devotional literature, much of which, especially the Gospels, she did read. These texts contained numerous examples of martyred women, sufferers who bore the travails of temporal existence while remaining true to their faith. All, like Labzina, embraced suffering in Christ's name, and they regularly looked to Mary, Holy Virgin and Mother of God, as their exemplar. The adoration of the Mother of God permeates Russian Orthodoxy, and it was common to pray to icons—sacred images—of Mary, asking her to protect and provide for the supplicant. Orthodox liturgy also includes prayers to Mary directly, and these offered direct models for empowerment and social engagement for holy and religious women. One popular religious tale, for example, *The Journey of the Mother of God through Hell* portrayed Mary as she wandered through the many layers of Hell, observing the suffering of the sinners and impious, and agreeing to intercede with God on their behalf:

> And a tormented one, seeing her, said, "How is it, Holy Virgin, that you have visited us? Your blessed Son came upon the earth

and did not ask us, nor did Abraham the Patriarch, nor Moses the Prophet, nor John the Baptist, nor Paul the Apostle, the favorite of the Lord. But you, most Holy Virgin, are an intercessor and protector for the Christian people. You have prayed to God for us."[10]

This image of the Holy Mother as the intercessor with God on behalf of the Christian people recurs in numerous religious lives, prayers, and lore. The sixteenth-century *Book of Household Management (Domostroi)* offers the following advice on prayer:

> "Lord Jesus Christ, Son of God, have mercy on me, a sinner."
> Say this prayer six hundred times. For the seven hundredth, pray to the Immaculate Virgin:
> "My Lady, Most Holy Mother of God, intercede for me, a sinner." Then go back to the beginning, and repeat this continually. If someone says these prayers needing Her help . . . at the end of the first year Jesus, Son of God, will rejoice in him. After the second year, the Holy Ghost will enter into him. . . .[11]

Although Labzina had probably never heard of *Domostroi,* its prescriptions recur in many other liturgical texts, which Labzina surely did know. And, in fact, she reproduces the model of Holy Mother/Holy Virgin as intercessor repeatedly in her memoir and transposes those very qualities to her own mother and to herself. Early in the memoir Labzina's dying mother proclaims, "If you are ever in a position to do good deeds for the poor and unfortunate, you shall be carrying out God's law, and peace will reign in your heart." Time and again Labzina portrays her mother, and later herself, as receiving the supplications of the poor and helpless (who unfailingly called the two women "mother") and then interceding on behalf of these poor people with powerful officials, wardens, and landlords. Indeed, it is her own success in interceding for prisoners in Nerchinsk that convinces Labzina she has come of age, that she is ready to accept the mantle of womanhood from her mother. "I fulfilled all of my mother's instructions here: I visited the ill and suffering every day and tended to them. . . .

Oh, how contented my heart was then." Thus, for Labzina, Mary provided the source par excellence of female empowerment, the moral basis for female social action in patriarchal Russia, a reconciliation between submissiveness on one hand and individuality on the other.

Mary's virginity also appears to have loomed large as an ideal for Labzina, albeit as a kind of asexuality. Nowhere in her memoir does she express, even obliquely, her own sexuality, though the sexual entanglements of others make up a large part of her narrative. When the subject does arise it is always in the context of depravity, specifically her husband's depravity. Karamyshev engaged in sex with loose women, young girls, and even his niece. He seems to have flirted with all manner of women, "pretty or ugly—it was all the same to him, so long as there was a woman around." But if he ever had sexual relations with his wife we never hear about it, and she was utterly repelled by his suggestions that she pursue intimate relations with other men who attracted her. The diary, too, avoids entirely the matter of physical affection between Anna and her second husband, Labzin.

If it is difficult to find immediate Russian antecedents that might have influenced Labzina in her writing, it is not hard to find analogous works by her contemporaries in other countries, pious women whose faith in God is sorely tested. Labzina could never have known these women or read their diaries, but the striking similarities between her concerns and theirs attest to a common source of inspiration with the Christian tradition of female suffering and devotion. According to Jane Rendall, when working-class women in Britain wrote about themselves, they most often told tales of self-abnegation and spiritual struggle. Their husbands were usually the focus of the struggle, as these women disputed codes of behavior, family resources, and religious values. "One notable source of conflict," Rendall writes, "emerges within the spiritual narrative, that between the converted wife and unredeemed husband."[12]

All these issues are, of course, central to Labzina's tale as well. Karamyshev gambled away their livelihood, advocated a kind of free love, and refused to partake of Christian ritual.

And though all Anna's moral precepts taught her not to complain of his behavior, for fear of hurting her own reputation along with his, by the time she wrote the memoir she clearly saw her story as an important moral lesson for others. For the British women, Rendall writes, moral education took on a central role and sometimes grew into a missionary impulse to "take these moral responsibilities into a wider world."[13] Labzina in her diary has reached a similar point, not exactly as a missionary, but in her role as a moral elder and example to the Masonic brotherhood and its circle. She draws lessons from her own memoir to apply to the lives of those around her later on, as with her comments about the marriage of Vera (her ward), or those about her friend and fellow Masonic wife, Andreevskaya (Dec. 4–5):

> I do not praise her for exposing her husband's great dishonesty. What will she accomplish by that, and how will she live with a dishonest husband after that? By revealing his dishonesty she loses her own reputation.

Since much of the memoir focused on the difficulty the young Anna had in not exposing her first husband's vices, this comment in the later diary shows her concern for passing on the hard lessons of her youth. (Though, of course, she does finally expose her husband's vices in her memoir, after his death.)

Even closer to Labzina's situation was the plight of Puritan women in New England. Their Calvinist tradition required of them the same sort of submission as Freemasonry did, and it set up a similar tension regarding the audacity of women's authorship. In both contexts a woman needed to have a significant moral message to justify writing at all, and it happened rarely. The diary of Abigail Abbot Bailey (1746–1815), an active member of the Church of Christ in New Hampshire, shows striking similarities to Labzina's memoir. When "the all-wise God" decides to give her a nonbelieving, philandering husband, Abigail Bailey keeps her sorrow to herself, occasionally pleads with him to change his ways, and expresses her complaints only in prayer. But when her husband chooses one of their daughters as the object of his lust, she can submit no longer. Like Labzina, she locates the point at which depravity is too extreme for the submissive woman's role to apply, and this frees her both to rebel and to write. (Like Labzina's memoir, Bailey's diary was published only after her death. It was left to a "minister of the Gospel and another gentleman of public education" to determine whether Bailey's diary should be published; they, not she, determined that the work would be of sufficient didactic value to make it worth bringing such horrors out in the open, "that the public might be benefited by them.")[14]

In Bailey's case, she wrote a diary of ongoing injustices, not an instructional memoir after the fact. She explicitly addresses her pen as an outlet for her anger and sorrow. At one point she writes, "May 26, 1774. I endeavored to console my afflicted heart with my pen, by writing as follows: 'Why art thou cast down O my soul?'"[15] Labzina never gives us similar insights into why she wrote the memoir, nineteen years after Karamyshev's death. In his introduction to the original (1903) edition, Modzalevsky suggests that her motive was "only a desire to recall her difficult past and . . . compare it with her happy present."[16]

Like the spiritual autobiographies of Bailey and others in the west, Labzina's memoir and diary give voice to a woman who had much to tell but was expected to keep her silence. For Bailey explicitly, and for Labzina as well, writing served as what Catriona Kelly has called "compensation for powerlessness."[17] By casting their sad tales of abuse as uplifting moral lessons, they found a way around the silence and into a broader spiritual sisterhood. Presumably, the intended readers of these works were primarily women, as guardians of the private sphere. Lonely as their lives were, the writers could take some comfort in the imagined companionship of future readers who would understand their plight. In Labzina's case the diary she wrote after her memoir is that much more poignant, because by then she seems to have forsworn even that imagined companionship. Forgetting the "dear friends" of her childhood—her mother, nanny, and mother-in-law—she now has adopted the Masons' negative view of women and rewritten her own past:

Never will man come to understand woman, with all the cunning and slyness of our sex, even if he knows her for twenty years. It only takes a month to figure out a man, but us—never. Forgive me, merciful God, for these thoughts, but I have the misfortune to know this from much experience: I've never been led astray by a man, whereas women have tried to cast me down into the abyss, and men have saved me. (October 3)

This from a woman whose first husband was a constant cipher to her and spared no efforts to "lead her astray." At the time she is writing this entry the brotherhood is collapsing and her husband Labzin is increasingly moody and difficult to talk to. Anna Evdokimovna has left herself no apparent outlets but the diary, which is addressed to no one but herself. If the memoir is a bold *cri de coeur* to an unseen sisterhood, the diary is a stifled cry that speaks volumes about the lonely lot of a devout woman among the cult of Freemasonry, whose attitude toward women was often demeaning.

LITERARY STYLE

The aesthetic model for Russian literature of Labzina's day was sentimentalism, which tried to replace neoclassicism with something lighter and more intimate, more in tune with European models of cultural refinement. Writers sought a language that was flexible and natural, eschewing stilted Slavonicisms and rigid literary hierarchies. As Judith Vowles writes, they moved their subject matter out of the public realm of official life into more private arenas, seeing the "fashionable Russian woman" as an ideal reader. At the same time, the Masonic movement rejected "fashionability" and refinement as worthy goals. Freemasons such as Kheraskov wrote allegorical works emphasizing moral messages, and their ideal reader was more the "intelligent" individual than the fashionable one.

In Labzina's writing we can see both impulses at work. The moral message is always present, and had she published the memoir in her lifetime, the fashionable reader would have found many cautions against pride, sloth, and sins of the flesh.

But there is no allegory here, only the intimate details of a family's life—her life, told in straightforward, conversational prose. Moreover, as a writer Labzina partakes of many of the stock conventions of sentimentalist prose. For a girl who was raised in Spartan conditions to be resilient and uncomplaining, she is remarkably prone to fainting fits and nervous illness. True, these fits come on not as a result of romantic passions but due to affronts to her Christian morality and (in the diary) threats to the unity of her husband's lodge. But they do appeal to a tender sensibility. This is especially true of the story of the cherry tree in her garden that spontaneously withers as Anna Evdokimovna prepares to move away. And though there are direct broadsides at refined sensibilities, these often read as the least natural elements of Labzina's style. A case in point is her dialogue with Kheraskov, as he tries to teach her that her love for his nephew is unseemly (60):

> "Doesn't it hurt you not to be able to love him this way?"
>
> "No, my father, I assure you that from now on I will be very careful not to disgrace myself, and not to lose your love. You have opened my eyes and now that I understand all this, it terrifies me to see that without your help I would not have seen this and would have brought misfortune on myself and maybe on my husband."

The language here is more stilted than in her other direct speech and has the quality of a written manual on behavior rather than a real conversation.

The sentimentalist leanings in her memoir point up a puzzle about how to classify Labzina as a writer. Her utter devotion to Freemasonry is clear, as acknowledged by the Masons themselves in their ceremony honoring her in 1821 (see appendix 1). But her actions, especially her writing, often depart from, and even subvert, the Masonic ideal of passive and obedient feminine virtue. Labzina does submit to her husband, is first and foremost a wife and helpmeet, and her writing serves moral, not aesthetic, purposes. But the very fact that she wrote a memoir is audacious, to use Barbara Heldt's term.[18] The famous Freemason, journalist, and publisher (and devoted correspondent of Labzina's husband) Nikolai Novikov (1744–1818) once commented that he opposed the notion of an "ideal female reader" on the grounds that women should be wives and mothers, not readers and writers. Labzina did not merely choose to write, she penned a document of her rebellion against her first husband, from her initial misgivings about the marriage to her efforts to separate from him.

She rebels, too, against the whole process of giving a young girl away in marriage and separating her from her own family, as well as against the way women are held to different rules than men. "Why didn't you tell me about any of this before my betrothal?" she asks a well-meaning aunt. "What kind of law is this—get married and lose everything that you hold dear? And how can it be that I must not share my love with my family! Why then don't I forbid him from loving his?" The unjust treatment of women in marriage is a constant subtext of the memoir. Although Anna bears the brunt of this injustice in her own (first) marriage, she does manage to mitigate its effects on others. When she is sixteen, for example, she finds an opportunity to prevent a friend her own age from being married off against her wishes.

The memoir must have afforded Anna some consolation, allowing her to spill out at long last the story of her early trials. This would run counter to her early lessons in humility and submissiveness, but it does accord with the picture of her that emerges in her diary. While she adopts mostly a confessional tone, large portions of the diary seem to serve primarily to vent her anger—at sister Alexandra Petrovna, at the lapsed brethren, at women's perfidy, at her own physical ailments. No small degree of pride is evident in both works. Though she rails against herself for vanity (first entry of the diary), she misses no opportunity to report other people's praise for her or to pass judgment on others. She is an "angel" many times over in the memoir, for example. And in the diary, she manages to do penance for her suspicious nature and to vent her suspicions, all in one remarkable sentence:

Now, Lord, I confess to you all my sins of the present month. I did nothing good for myself or for others and was constantly in doubt on all sides and suspicious of Yuliana Egorovna; and she did nothing but lie in every word she said, like some sort of traitor—and many falsehoods came out; but I still do not want to believe it, and God grant that everything I hear about her is untrue. I'm very sorry for her. (October 30)

In short, what emerges in the memoir and diary is a portrait of a real person in all her contradictory nature: submissive and rebellious, ashamed of her pridefulness and proud of her self-abnegation, spiteful and judgmental and meek and conciliatory. For a woman of character in an abusive marriage and, later, ensconced in a male-centered religious cult, writing turns out to be Labzina's only recourse. Only the written medium can embrace her paradoxical impulses to tell and not to tell, to preach loving acceptance while harboring hatred and anger. It is easy to imagine her recording her private thoughts, ostensibly for herself alone, while secretly hoping others would read them some day.

Powerless as she feels she is to change her circumstances, she still uses nearly every entry to complain about her health, her family's finances, and the behavior of those around her. She also tries to apply the hard-won lessons of her youth to her current situation. She wants to protect young Vera Alexandrovna from the loneliness and helplessness of an unhappy marriage ("Why force her? It will happen of its own accord; there's no need to take that little pleasure away from her now . . ." [Nov. 17–18]). As Heldt puts it (perhaps a bit too strongly), "There is a sense of her own self-worth that never fails Labzina: the very act of writing pages that dwell on misery testifies to an ability to confront shame and horror" (78–79).

There is a danger in overemphasizing the rebellious nature of Labzina's writing. She herself probably did not see it that way; at most she used her writing as a private means of venting emotions she did not feel free to express aloud. Although she models some degree of toughness in the face of hardship, both by resisting Karamyshev's depravities and by writing her own life, Labzina is by no means a liberated woman. For all of her self-righteousness, most of the moral message of Labzina's memoir is about obedience and submission. The girl's various mentors all caution her to give her husband no cause for displeasure, to keep his failings to herself, to accept God's will gladly. In the diary the older Labzina repeatedly expresses the wish to protect her husband from aggravation or scandal, and when she attempts to give him advice she comes to regret it:

> Last night my husband said to me, "Thank you for instructing me and teaching me, but I know what I am doing." I reproached myself inside for being unable to hold my tongue. (December 10–18)

Perhaps the diary is her way of helping herself "hold her tongue" around others.

One of the most important morals of Labzina's writing is her belief that her personal victories and ultimate sense of independence, too, come through submission. Time and again Karamyshev must admit that his young wife has not merited his anger but has defended his honor rather than impugning it. Her forbearance always restores her to his good graces, and it seems to be what endears her to others as well. Finally, the crowning event of Labzina's life, when her husband's lodge presented her with the Masonic gloves, was above all a tribute to her sense of virtue and duty. Still, the modern reader cannot help sensing that her writing serves to negate that message of submission. There is a quality of vengeance here, or at least of getting the last laugh. Riddled as these writings are with pious homilies about obedience and marital duty, the memorable passages are those that make us feel the injustice and hardship she endured. And not just for us as readers: Anna herself seems to have retained the most vivid memories of those very injustices to which she believed she had gladly submitted.

LANGUAGE

There is a lively freshness, or naïveté, about Labzina's writing, and her language provides insight into the everyday vernacular of educated but provincial Russian women of her time. Except in her most pious moments, there is little in Labzina's language to suggest an elevated or literary style. At least in terms of lexicon, her written language probably approximates the way she spoke. Her vocabulary and syntax are fairly simple, and there is abundant evidence of colloquialisms. She tends to use run-on sentences with relatively few participles and more parataxis (simple juxtaposition of descriptors) than is normal in more standard written diction:

> Instead of leaving in the morning as was normal, we set off at night when everyone was asleep, and no one saw our departure but my poor, sad nanny, who was more dead than alive as she parted with me, her face was terribly pale. (39)

She frequently uses emphatic interjections or the particle *i* ("And so . . .") to begin a story. She is also partial to repetitive phrasings (*rodnykh ne bylo nikogo* 'there were no relatives, no one' rather than the standard *rodnykh ne bylo* 'there were no relatives'), dashes, and other interruptions. For example,

> I sat by the window, thinking—what, I didn't know myself: I did wonder about my mother, whether she was alive, but took comfort knowing she was not alone. (29)

For all its simplicity, Labzina's style is richly variable, especially when she reports dialogue. In recounting direct speech she makes broad use of the markers of spoken language, such as particles (*zhe, a, to,* in addition to the ubiquitous *i*), dashes, exclamations, and introductory phrases (*akh* 'oh,' *kazhetsia* 'it seems,' *ved'* 'after all,' *net* 'no,' *vot* 'here, so,' *izvol'* 'please'). She also makes some effort to give people distinctive voices, using dialect and even idiolect. At one point Anna Evdokimovna seeks the help of an elderly Polish acquaintance, I. O. Golynski, to take her on an outing against her husband's wishes. His dialogue is marked with Polonisms (he calls her *pania,* Labzina's fractured rendering of the Polish *pani,* for "lady," and uses the Polish *dobrze,* 'good'), mispronunciations *(dak, koneshno),* and non-native syntax. Later, when she is living among convicts in Siberia, she reports their speech, too, with distinctive qualities. The former robber and murderer speaks with a brutal direct-ness. ("I was a robber and plied the Volga for seventeen years. What I liked best was to stab people like me and leave them barely alive—and seeing them writhe gave me joy."[91]) The former nobleman has a more elevated style: "How could I ex-pect such a merciful visitation in my unfortunate circum-stances?" (92).

As a storyteller, Labzina also has a certain gift for the dra-matic. She uses dialogue to good effect and reveals only as much information as she might have had at the time, so that the reader shares her suspense. For example, when two hun-dred Tatars come to claim her mother's land, the mother chal-lenges them as to why they want to dispossess her and her children. Labzina reports, "They began to speak among them-selves, but my mother could not make out what they were say-ing." When finally they embrace her mother, it comes as a sur-prise. Similarly, her initial innocence about Karamyshev's philandering is convincing. After she naively tells her nanny that she has just seen Karamyshev sleeping "in a friendly em-brace" with his niece, the nanny says,

> "Don't tell your husband that you went to their room during the night."
>
> "Why not?" I asked, surprised. "I can't keep anything from him. In fact, I already told him."
>
> "You didn't say that I know, did you?"
>
> "No!"
>
> "Then I beg you not to, if you love me."
>
> I looked at her and said, "My God, how you all torment me!" (30)

In this short dialogue we get a clear picture of the various conflicting perspectives: the trusting young girl who believes she must always tell the truth, but is learning otherwise; the nanny who is trying to protect her—and herself; and the un-scrupulous and potentially vengeful husband as well. We come

to understand how the girl is hemmed in not only by her unhappy marriage but by the strictures on knowledge and speech
that her supposed friends and mentors have given her. Dialogue becomes not just a storytelling device but a way of providing a foreground for and exploring social conventions.

In literary terms, the least effective sections are the ones
Labzina herself probably saw as most important: the didactic
sermons and Socratic dialogues with which her various teach-
ers favor her at regular intervals. One after another they ad-
monish her to be obedient, not to complain about her husband's failings, and to put her faith in God. The language of all
these sermons is remarkably similar, rather bookish and stilted.
It does not have the ring of truth present in so much of her
other narration, perhaps because the gist of each admonition is
that she should love her husband above all others, which to a
modern reader may sound implausible.

This is not to say that Labzina is insincere in these didactic
sections. In fact, their style comes closest to that of the diary,
which she presumably wrote for herself alone. The diary has
little of the dialogue and storytelling of the memoir, and more
prayer and moral reflection. Labzina uses shorthand and ellipti-
cal comments to refer to things only she may have known, but
even in her private language she observes strict proprieties,
adopting an elevated tone to address God and refusing to
name the embarrassing malady (most likely diarrhea) that af-
flicts her. Still, when she does narrate events or dialogues, the
language is simple and conversational, much like that of the
memoir.

In the end, one is continually struck by the conflict between
the awkwardness of her writing, her bad grammar and diction,
on the one hand, and her deftness at directing, or even manip-
ulating, the reader on the other. Certain key words—for example, the reference to her mother as "birth mother" or "progenitress" (*roditelnitsa* in Russian)—seem to jump off the page with
emotional content, and the entirety of her texts is suffused
with a bitterness that is often overpowering. Other terms are
subtler and seem to imply both a surface meaning and a more
judgmental secondary one. The discussion of Karamyshev's

niece is a good example of this. Labzina can barely bring herself to write the niece's name, and instead refers to her by initials, "V.A.," or abbreviations, "Vera Alek.," almost as if to imply that she would choke on the full name. Here and elsewhere Labzina employs a word for maiden *("devka")* in a way that hints simultaneously at both innocence and debauchery without explicitly stating either. One can well imagine that there was much in Labzina's daily life that was happy or mundane, even perhaps during her first marriage. But, if so, she studiously avoids mentioning it except in passing and chooses instead to dwell on the pain and unhappiness of private life. One suspects, then, that the act of writing was her way of taking revenge, leaving written evidence to be discovered by others after she was gone. A last laugh, so to speak, in which her defiance consisted in writing the definitive tale of her first marriage, long after Karamyshev could reply.

In contrast to the memoir, whose language flows rather easily, the diary poses some challenges to the modern reader. The thoughts it contains are intensely private, and they assume an intimate familiarity with early-nineteenth-century Freemasonry and its leading personalities. The full diary is filled with obscure and highly particular references to rites, personal rivalries, and insider gossip, all of which was intensely important to Labzina, but much less so to the modern reader, who would require voluminous annotations merely to keep the characters straight. We have abridged the diary extensively, therefore, cutting out most of the references to individuals and to arcane Masonic ritual.

Freemasonry arrived in Russia some time in the 1730s, imported probably by Englishmen who had come to serve in the Russian army or to engage in trade. According to Douglas Smith, the number of lodges grew rapidly, from fewer than fourteen in the late 1760s to about ninety in the late 1780s, with a combined membership of as many as two thousand at any one time.[19] Approximately two-thirds of the lodges were established in Moscow or St. Petersburg, the two leading cities of the empire, but several towns in the western borderlands, including Riga, Vilno, and Reval housed two or more lodges each. Lodges also sprang up in about ten provincial Russian towns.

Although membership rolls included representatives of various social strata, the Masonic milieu, at least in Russia, was overwhelmingly noble, a fact that is reflected in its cosmopolitan setting and in the leisurely sociability described in Labzina's diary. Many, perhaps most, lodges functioned primarily as social clubs, in which nominal devotion to improvement of the mind and spirit coexisted with informal conviviality. Labzina's diary provides a glimpse into this side of Masonic culture, as lodge members—the "brothers"—gathered several times per month, and seemingly for hours on end (just count the number of references to "pleasant evenings" and leisurely dinners in the diary), for little purpose other than to share each other's company, chat, and discuss the issues of the day.

Labzina abhorred this merely social activity, deeming it frivolous, even corrupt, a "republic of individuals" rather than a brotherhood. In truth, her husband's lodge, Dying Sphinx, was renowned as the most religious and spiritual of Russia's lodges, and it is this religious quality that resonates in the diary. Masonic ritual was constructed around a strict hierarchy, one which observed a sharp dichotomy between the society at large (public, unconscious, morally undirected) and the existence behind the closed doors of the lodge (private, secret, fraternal, and devoted to inner enlightenment). Much of Labzina's diary bemoans what she perceives as the loss of these special values, the pollution of the inner sanctum by the world at large. In a couple of passages she imagines this as foretokening the end of days, the looming apocalypse that would precede the Second Coming.

Once inside the lodge, the hierarchy intensified through a series of five concentric circles, or orders. To move from an outer circle to an inner one required passing a test of faith and virtue, followed by a secret oath, and then a literal passage into a sanctum from which most masons were excluded. The majority of lodges included only two or three orders, but Dying Sphinx embraced all five, a reflection of its commitment to spirituality. As the elected Grand Master of the lodge, Alexander Labzin occupied the highest order, and along with his two wardens (one junior, one senior), he was responsible for keeping order and moral cohesion among all the lodge members.[20]

At the time of the diary, Dying Sphinx's inner harmony had deteriorated as a result of personal rivalries and disagreements over the true mission of the lodge. ("It is no longer a peaceful union, it is now a stormy sea" [119]) Labzin's notoriously abrasive personality and his imperious manner contributed mightily to the disharmony, but in Labzina's diary we see none of this. Instead, we are told of bad faith, failed loyalty, two-facedness, conspiracy, and insufficient love ("they use my husband's good heart to evil purposes" [119]). How, she asks repeatedly, can the brothers be so disrespectful of her husband, who embodies the highest human virtues and who has done so much good for them. Her only answer, as we see, is human weakness, and as in her memoir, she finds solace and meaning only in her faith and her powerful and inscrutable God ("Lord, I will seek out You alone and open my whole heart to You and fill myself with You" [118])

Taken together, the memoir and diary give us a good sense of the three main strata of language usage of Labzina's social milieu: conversational speech, simple expository prose, and the more elevated tones of prayer and piety. In translation, of course, these strata will be less differentiated than in the Russian, and there are no doubt many places where we have standardized the language in favor of getting the sense across, for which we apologize. We also have taken the liberty of dividing the memoir into seven chapters instead of presenting it as one long narrative the way Labzina herself did.

. . .

TRANSLITERATION

In transliterating Russian words and names into English we have followed the U. S. Library of Congress transliteration system. The one exception is in proper names beginning with a vowel such as "ia" or "iu," where, for ease of reading in the text, we have used "Y" instead of "I" (Yakovlev, Yaroslavl).

NOTES

1. A state counselor ranked relatively highly in Russia's governmental service, entitling the holder to be a hereditary nobleman and to receive a fairly high salary. Yakovlev retired with that title, an indication that this was the highest he had risen in state service. A state counselor typically would be a senior staff member in the civil administration, almost certainly working in St. Petersburg, probably in one of the administrative "colleges" that had been organized in 1722.

2. Durova's memoir is available in an English translation. See Nadezhda Durova, *The Cavalry Maiden: Journals of a Russian Officer in the Napoleonic Wars,* trans. Mary Zirin (Bloomington, Ind.: Indiana University Press, 1989).

3. This, too, is available in English. See Ekaterina Dashkova, *The Memoirs of Princess Dashkova,* trans. and ed. Kyril Fitzlyon, intro. Jehanne M. Gheith (Durham, N.C.: Duke University Press, 1995).

4. Catherine II, *The Memoirs of Catherine the Great,* trans. Moura Budberg (London: Hamish Hamilton, 1955).

5. V. M. Kabuzan, *Narody Rossii v XVIII veke. Chislennost' i etnicheskii sostav* (Moscow: Nauka, 1990), 230.

6. The *terem* was the secluded area in which Muscovite elite women were obligated to stay, physically removed from men. The *terem* was formally abolished during the reign of Peter the Great.

7. A. G. Tartakovskii, *Russkaia memuaristika XVIII–pervoi poloviny XIX v.* (Moscow: Nauka, 1991), 244-70.

8. V. M. Bokova, "Tri zhenschiny," in *Istoriia zhizni blagorodnoi zhenshchiny,* ed. V. M. Bokova (Moscow: Novoe literaturnoe obozrenie, 1996), 5.

9. There is an English translation of Avvakum's autobiography, *The Life of the Archpriest Avvakum by Himself,* trans. Jane Harrison and Hope Mirrlees (London: L. and V. Woolf, 1924). A more recent translation is found in *Anthology of Russian Literature from the Earliest Writings to Modern Fiction,* ed. Nicholas Rzhevsky (Armonk, N.Y.: M. E. Sharpe, 1996).

10. This tale has been translated into English in *Medieval Russia's Epics, Chronicles, and Tales,* ed. Serge A. Zenkovsky (New York: Dutton, 1963), 122-29.

11. *The Domostroi: Rules for Russian Households in the Time of Ivan the Terrible,* ed. and trans. Carolyn Johnston Pouncy (Ithaca: Cornell Univeristy Press, 1994), 89.

12. Jane Rendall, "'A Short Account of My Unprofitable Life':

Autobiographies of Working Class Women in Britain, c. 1775–1845," in *Women's Lives/Women's Times: New Essays on Autobiography,* ed. Trev Lynn Broughton and Linda Anderson (Albany: State University of New York Press, 1997), 41.

13. Ibid., 38.

14. From the advertisement to the original publication, reprinted in *Religion and Domestic Violence in Early New England: The Memoirs of Abigail Abbot Bailey,* ed. Ann Taves (Bloomington, Ind.: Indiana University Press, 1989), 52. An echo of this is heard in Sergei Ol'denburg's preface to the 1914 edition of Labzina's memoirs, in which he draws instructive comparisons "between the 'rules' of the past and the present-day rejection of obligations and duty in favor of self-assertion and worship of one's own 'I,'" *Vospominaniia Anny Evdokimovny Labzinoi, 1758–1828* (St. Petersburg: Tipografiia B. M. Vol'fa, 1914), iv.

15. Taves, ed., *Religion and Domestic Violence,* 62.

16. B. L. Modzalevskii, "Predislovie," to A. E. Labzina, *Vospominaniia* (St. Petersburg: Tipografiia B. M. Vol'fa, 1914), 13.

17. Catriona Kelly, *A History of Russian Women's Writing 1820–1992* (Oxford: Clarendon Press, 1992), 22.

18. Barbara Heldt, *Terrible Perfection* (Bloomington: Indiana University Press, 1987), 66.

19. Douglas Smith, *Working the Rough Stone: Freemasonry and Society in Eighteenth-Century Russia* (DeKalb, Ill.: Northern Illinois University Press, 1999), 19.

20. For more on the structure and organization of Russian lodges, see Smith, 18–52.

REFERENCES

Bokova, V. M. "Tri zhenshchiny." Introduction to *Istoriia zhizni blagorodnoi zhenshchiny,* ed. V. M. Bokova, 5–12. Moscow: Novoe literaturnoe obozrenie, 1996.

Golovina, V. N. "Memuary" (c. 1817). In *Istoriia zhizni blagorodnoi zhenshchiny,* ed. V. M. Bokova, 89–339. Moscow: Novoe literaturnoe obozrenie, 1996.

Heldt, Barbara. *Terrible Perfection.* Bloomington, Ind.: Indiana University Press, 1987.

Kelly, Catriona. *A History of Russian Women's Writing 1820–1992.* Oxford: Clarendon Press, 1994.

Rendall, Jane. "'A Short Account of My Unprofitable Life': Autobiographies of Working Class Women in Britain, c. 1775–1845."

In *Women's Lives/Women's Times: New Essays on Autobiography,* ed. Trev Lynn Broughton and Linda Anderson, 31–50. Albany, N.Y.: State University of New York Press, 1997.

Smith, Douglas. *Working the Rough Stone: Freemasonry and Society in Eighteenth-Century Russia.* DeKalb, Ill.: Northern Illinois University Press, 1999.

Taves, Ann, ed. *Religion and Domestic Violence in Early New England: The Memoirs of Abigail Abbot Bailey.* Bloomington, Ind.: Indiana University Press, 1989.

Taves, Ann. "Self and God in the Early Published Memoirs of New England Women." In *American Women's Autobiography,* ed. Margo Culley, 57–74. Madison: University of Wisconsin Press, 1992.

Vowles, Judith. "The 'Feminization' of Russian Literature: Women, Language, and Literature in Eighteenth-Century Russia." In *Women Writers in Russian Literature,* ed. Toby W. Clyman and Diana Greene, 35–54[?]. Westport, Conn., and London: Greenwood Press, 1994.

DAYS OF A RUSSIAN NOBLEWOMAN

The Memoir

~ I ~

I lost my father when I was five years old, and, as a conse-
quence, I barely remember him.[1] I had two younger brothers.
The youngest I loved with a passion, the elder not so much,
because of his harsh character. My mother was thirty-one
when my father died; she had loved him deeply and was in despair at his loss. In her grief she grumbled endlessly at God—
this is how she put it herself. Finally despair had such an effect
on her that she began to fantasize that my father would appear
to her and he would tell her not to leave the village under any
pretext and not to allow anyone in to see her, not even the
children, otherwise he would stop coming to her. She
promised him everything and lay in her room with the windows shut. She spoke to him constantly and was so content
that she forgot about us entirely and seemed not to know that
she had children. So, we were left in the care of an aunt.

For a long while we were not cognizant of my mother's
frightful condition, we just thought that she was delirious. At
last my nanny began to observe her, and she grew suspicious
because [mother] was not admitting anyone in to see her and
kept asking to be left alone, "and if I need something I will
call." Finally nanny began to eavesdrop by the doors, and she

heard a conversation, she even heard my father's name, heard my mother call him to sit by her side and say, "You won't ever leave me? I have abandoned everything for you, even the children." But she heard no answer from him.

Having overheard this scene, my nanny approached my aunt in horror and recounted what she'd seen. My aunt didn't believe her, and she went to determine for herself whether it was true. They did not know where to begin. They tried several times to persuade [my mother] to allow someone to sit with her, but they were unable to. Finally, she began to speak openly about it herself, and she declared that she wasn't alone. "I am with my husband." They tried to explain to her that this was impossible, that the deceased do not walk, but that only threw her into a rage. There were no relatives around, since they all lived far away, and this state of affairs continued for about three years.

Everyone around us was praying for her, and they made us do it too, but we did not know for whom we were praying because we never saw her. She came to hate us and she could not bear to hear our names, and would only say, "They bother me most of all." At last, fortunately for us and for her, my uncle returned from St. Petersburg and he came straightaway to the village and saw my mother in this frightful state.[2] He began to call her by name and ordered the windows to be opened, and he wouldn't leave her. All this sent her into such a powerful rage that she threw herself upon my uncle and cursed him, while trying to scratch and bite him. But uncle ordered that the horses and servants be readied, and he told her that he was going to take her away at once. She begged him not to separate her from her friend, but my uncle took her in his arms, carried her out and placed her in a carriage. He sat himself at the driver's seat, and he placed the servants on the other side. She cried out so much that it was horrible to hear. He drove her to town and took her directly to his house.

For the next six weeks my aunt, uncle, and a priest did not leave her side. Talking with her was impossible. She didn't listen and she didn't answer, but they read the Gospels endlessly and talked among themselves. For four weeks she didn't say a word and seemed to see nothing, but suddenly one night she leapt up, started to pray, and asked the priest to give her the Eucharist straight away, a task which he happily carried out.[3] After this she began to cry and asked them to bring us there so she could see us. This request made everyone around her so glad that they sent for us then and there. Meanwhile, she recounted that in a dream a wise man had visited her and commenced scolding her for having committed such a terrible crime against God. How could she think that her husband was visiting her?

"If you only knew what kind of spirit you were talking to, you would be horrified. I shall show you." And then I saw a horrible monster. "Here is your interlocutor, for whom you have forsaken God and your first responsibility, your children." She fell at his feet and cried out, "Help me, a sinner, to seek forgiveness for my crime. I promise from this minute to serve my God. I shall comfort the lowly, the infirm, and the suffering, and I shall help them." He answered, "Behold, do these things and they will expiate your crime. Right now ask the good shepherd to administer the holy sacraments. Do you have any idea how long you have deprived yourself of this precious gift? Know that your precious good deeds were recalled before the Heavenly Father, and the prayers of your family and friends, and of the innocent orphans you abandoned, reached His throne, and you are returning now to repent and to minister to the unfortunate."[4]

At last she recognized this elder as her own father. She cried out, and then she awoke. They brought us and we saw before us a tender mother who showered us with her tears, led us to our uncle and said, "This is your father and benefactor. He is returning your mother to you, and you are orphans no more." So she moved back into her own home and found nothing out of order there, because those upon whom the responsibility had fallen had carried it out to the letter as if she had always been there. In the village as well, through the kind and diligent oversight of the caretaker, my mother found everything so well stocked with more cattle and fowl than she had ever expected. Now that her affairs in town had been arranged, she went with us to the village, and here we began our upbringing.

I was already seven years old and had studied my ABCs,[5] but my mother herself taught me to write, and she began to educate my heart, greatly with words, and doubly so by example. She devoted herself to the well-being of our peasants, who idolized her. When someone happened to fall ill in the village, my mother, eschewing medical assistance, treated all the illnesses herself, and God assisted her. She sat with the desperately ill for days on end, and I would be there with her and carry out her orders for serving the sick as best I could, given my age. At night she dispatched my nanny, who willingly did everything that she was ordered to do. She was always there when someone was dying, and I would be at her side, and throughout their final sufferings she prayed, sobbing, while kneeling before the cross. If the dying person was still conscious, she reassured him and comforted him with the hope of our Savior. In this way the sick were put at ease so that they could await their death with less fear.

Often in such circumstances she prevailed upon me to read about the passion of Christ the Savior, which gave extraordinary comfort to the sick. Wherever she went she brought the peace and blessing of God with her. As the neighbors came to understand that my mother was a healer, they began to bring sick people to her, and she never turned them away, and with gladness accepted all of them, and only very rarely did they die. Meanwhile, she taught me various handicrafts, and she fortified my body with a strict diet, and she kept me outdoors regardless of the weather. I had no fur coat for the winter, and I wore nothing on my legs but knitted stockings and boots. During the harshest frosts she would send me out on foot, and my only warmth came from a flannel housecoat. If my stockings got wet from the snow, she would have me keep them on, saying, "they'll dry on your legs." In the summer they would wake me up when the sun had barely risen and take me to bathe in the river. Back at home I would get a breakfast of hot milk and black bread. Tea was unknown to us.[6] After this I had to read the Holy Scripture and then get to work.

After bathing we immediately began our prayers, turning to the east and kneeling. Nanny and I read morning prayers, and how sweet it was then to pray with an innocent heart! And at those times I loved my Maker, although I knew little of [Christian] enlightenment. I kept being told that God is present everywhere and that He sees, knows, and hears, and no secret deed remains unrevealed to Him, so I was very afraid that I would do something bad. But the tender care of my benevolent and good nanny saved me from foolish deeds.

My mother gave us some time for games in the summer and taught us how to run. By the time I was ten I was so strong and agile that now I don't know even fifteen-year-old boys who are as strong as I was then. My high spiritedness was a source of distress for my honorable mother, however. My favorite activities were running and climbing trees, and no matter how tall a tree might be I would certainly climb it. When they punished me for doing this, I would sneak out quietly into the woods and do whatever I wished. At times I would bring my brothers along with me and teach them how to climb as well. This got our teacher into a lot of trouble.

My diet consisted of cabbage soup, kasha, and occasionally a piece of salted fish, and in the summer, greens and dairy.[7] During fasts, especially during Lent, there was not even fish. Even the coarsest food was part of our diet. In the mornings, instead of tea we got hot or whisked grape juice. Several people asked my mother why she was giving me such a crude upbringing, but she always responded, "I don't know what her circumstances will be. Perhaps she will be poor, or she might marry someone with whom she will be obliged to travel. In that case she will not pester her husband, she will not know what caprice is, and she will be satisfied with anything. She will be able to endure anything, be it cold or filth, and she won't catch colds. If she ends up rich, then it will be easy for her to grow accustomed to the good life." It was as if she had foreseen my fate, which held all these things in store for me.

She would haul me twenty versts[8] in a peasant wagon, making me travel on top, and in the fields I had to walk on foot, also for ten versts. Once we would get to where the reaping was taking place I would be hungry, and she would have them give us some peasant black bread and water, which I would eat with as much gusto as if we were dining at a grand table. She set the example herself by eating with me, and then we would go back on foot.

We sometimes arranged festive days for the peasants in the village. We would place tables in the middle of the courtyard. My mother would serve the peasants herself, and she would have us bring them beer and wine. When they returned home I would lead them to the gates and wish them good night, and they would bless me. Very often mother herself went with me to the bathing area, and she would look out with reverence at the sunrise and relate to me the majesty of God, as much as I could comprehend at that time. She even taught me to swim in the deep section of the river. She did not want me to be afraid of anything, and at the age of eleven I could swim across a wide and deep river without any help. I went boating in lakes and I steered the boats myself, and I worked in the garden and weeded, planted, and watered the beds by myself. My mother and I shared the work, thus lightening those burdens that were beyond what I could get done alone. She never made me do anything that she didn't do herself.

In wintertime we would travel to town where there were other lessons to learn. Each week I went with her to the prisons,[9] and mother and I handed out money, shirts, stockings, caps, robes, all this made with our own hands. If she came upon sick people she ministered to them, brought them tea and fed it to them herself, or more often had me do it. Together we would wash their wounds and bandage them. As soon as we showed our faces in the prison everyone would shout out and reach out their arms toward us, especially the infirm. Every day we provided food for the prison, and especially light fare for those who were ill. Every week we fed the destitute at home, and we served them right at the table. As they departed she would distribute money, shirts, stockings, and boots to everyone, or to be more precise, to whoever needed them, and not a single poor person was left without her assistance.

There was a man at our house whose job it was to seek out the poor and suffering, and he faithfully fulfilled this responsibility.[10] My mother was often ill herself, and at those times I visited the poor and the prison along with my nanny, and we carried out her responsibilities and cared for the sick as she prescribed. Whenever someone died in prison our servants were sent to cleanse the body, and we paid for the funeral ourselves. For the grievously ill she went to the prison with the pastor who had saved her. Together they would carry out their Christian obligation. She often sat with the pastor in the prison deep into the night, and they read, and talked with those who were ill. Frequently the convicts confessed their sins in the presence of all of them, and this eased their consciences. At these moments a joy radiated from her face, and she would embrace me and say, "If you ever are in a position to do good deeds for the poor and unfortunate, you shall be carrying out God's law, and peace will reign in your heart. God will anoint his blessing upon your head, and your wealth will multiply, and you shall be happy. If you are poor and have nothing to give, then couch your refusal with love so that your refusal will not anger the unfortunate. Even for your refusal you shall be blessed, and even in your poverty you can do good: visit the sick, console the suffering and discouraged. Always remember that they are as close to you as brothers, and for them you shall be rewarded by the Heavenly King. Remember, my friend, not to forget your mother's instructions."

Quite often they would bring a gang of convicts bound by a rope, with irons on their hands and feet. They would let my mother know that some convicts had come from prison. She would immediately go out, taking us with her. She would bring them everything they needed and sew linen cuffs for the irons, which otherwise chafed their arms and legs right down to the bone. If she noticed that the convicts were in a particularly bad state and weak, she would ask the supervisors to hand them over to her and she would immediately set about tending to their wounds. The supervisors never refused her because they all loved and respected her. And how many poor households were sustained by her, how many poor orphans she gave away in marriage! In short, she devoted her entire life to Christian duties.

She sent my brothers to one of her dearest acquaintances for their education, but my elder brother's stubborn character greatly angered her and she severely punished him. He was eight years old when our one benefactor, General Irman,[11] came to town on his way to taking the position of chief administrator in Barnaul.[12] Because he loved my mother so much he persuaded her to hand my brother over to him. She consented at once and trusted him as a friend. She was not mistaken. He took the place of father and mother [for my brother], and loved him like a son and made a man of him. But though my brother's character was tempered, it remained hard. But my younger brother had the most humble and quiet character, and everyone loved him, especially me. It seemed to me that the two of us had but a single soul, a single heart. When something made him unhappy, or if he wasn't learning his lessons and thereby angered my mother and the teacher, I felt such torment in my own heart it seemed I couldn't suffer as much on my own behalf. All of my joy was in his joy, and he repaid me in kind. He would look into my eyes and would know what I wanted.

I will say further about myself that I had very little will of my own. I wished only to be of use to my dear and esteemed mother. I do not remember ever failing to carry out her orders joyfully, and for that reason I was her favorite, although she did not often display much affection. For that very reason I valued her expressions of affection all the more when she caressed me for doing some good deed. Tears of joy would flow from me and I would kiss my mother's hand and kneel down before her. She would bless me and say, "My child, always be like this."

I loved my esteemed nanny no less, because I spent more time with her. Since the management of the villages relied entirely on my mother, her activities demanded much of her time and frequently took her away from me.[13] So nanny took her place. Her good examples and tireless vigilance affected me not only in my daily activities, but even in my sleep. The next day she would ask me, "Why did you sleep so fitfully today? Apparently yesterday your soul was not in order, or did you fail to carry out some of your responsibilities? Think, dear one, and tell me. Together we shall pray and ask the Heavenly Father to save you from all that could lead you to ruin!"

I would tearfully confess everything to her immediately and ask her to pray with me and for me at once, and to ask our Maker to forgive me. When we finished our prayers I would hug her and say that now I felt very cheerful and light. She would instruct me to be wary of anything that could burden my conscience, and she showed me several unfortunate examples that affected me greatly. She made it so that I never had a thought that wasn't open to her. She gave me resolutions for a great many things, and provided me with some thoughts to discuss with my mother. For me this was not a burden. This humble benefactress of mine had children of her own, but she was unstinting in carrying out her obligation to raise me. Her children were provided other women to look after them, and my own mother kept an eye on them and kept them near her own room.

[Nanny] and I would frequently go into the fields with our work, and she would ask me,

"Do you marvel at God's wisdom and do you gaze upon all of His works with respect? Do you see how He loves humanity, making all of creation for us, both for sustenance and for pleasure. Man himself was created in His image and likeness. Is it possible for us to live in a manner so that we would not strive to be like Him in all things? And is it possible not to love Him above all else and not to give thanks for all these kindnesses that He bestows upon us? You are especially obliged to give thanks for His unstinting kindnesses toward you, for granting you such a mother, who loves you and wants to bring you happiness by her good example and instruction. Just obey her and carry out her will, and I, too, her helper in your upbringing, also want every good thing for you. As far as my strength permits, and with God's help, I will instruct you as much as I know how. I thank God that you listen to me and love me; this alone is the reward I expect from you. There can be no greater good for me than to see you be like your dear mother.

"You don't remember your father.[14] He, too, was an exceptionally good man, and, as he lay dying, he said, 'Raise my children to know God, teach them from early childhood to love Him with all their heart, to love and honor their mother, to have respect and honor for their elders, not only those of equal standing, but also good servants. Teach them to love the poor and unfortunate. Do not accustom them to luxury, but rather to want.' He then turned to me and said, 'My friend Konstantinovna, promise me at the end of my life that you will carry out all of this and let me die in peace. My daughter has been in your care from birth, so of course you will not abandon her, and you will thus repay us for the love we have shown you.'

"I fell on my knees before him and kissed his hand, which had already begun to turn cold, and I swore that I would carry out everything. But your mother was not there, as she was already in bed in another room. He gathered up his strength to raise himself up so that he could embrace me, and he said, 'I thank you, my friend, for easing my final minutes. I want to request one more thing regarding my daughter. Great difficulties await her in her life. Pray for her. Stay by my wife's side. I have confidence in you in all of these matters that you will bring her comfort. Now go and let me be. Bring in the children so that I can bless them.'

"I went and, after waiting a bit, brought you. He gave his blessing, and once he asked the Heavenly Father to bless you, he said, 'My Lord! If they are going to live virtuously, then grant them your help. But if not, take them while they are still innocent.' And when he finished this, he said, 'I have done my duty. Now I must prepare myself for my own journey. Leave me.' And so we left sobbing. He lived one more day after this and thought of nothing except preparing himself. Up until the very last minute of his life he was completely conscious. His face showed contentment, and neither fear nor horror was apparent. His last words were, 'I give myself over to Your solemn mercy, my Savior! Receive my spirit and forgive me. Support those who remain after me and grant them the strength once I am gone not to curse or be angry at You.' He crossed himself and said something more, but so quietly that we couldn't hear it. And then he passed away. It was a great loss for all of us. He was a father and friend to us, and it seemed that all our hopes and joys died with him."

After she finished she cried bitterly and clasped me to her and said, "My child, be virtuous like your parents, and help me in my work, so that I may stand with you before the Heavenly Father without trembling and say joyfully, 'Here is the pledge her parents entrusted to me.'"

When she taught me to embroider she said, "Apply yourself, dear mother. Perhaps your labors will be necessary later in your life. If God finds it useful for you to experience poverty, then by knowing various handicrafts you will not suffer privation, you will earn your bread in an honest way, and you will remain joyful.[15] If your heart remains pure and your conscience is not troubled in any way, your burdens will seem light, and you will give thanks to your Lord for everything."

My happy life proceeded in this way until I was thirteen, and I was dearly loved by all my relatives. No one believed that I was only thirteen, and they all said that I was already sixteen.

My mother lived extraordinarily serenely. Just one thing worried her. Tatars[16] had risen up against her and wanted to take over our land as if it did not belong to her. One landlord, Kleopin, lived about five versts away from us, and he came by and told my mother that she should hasten to leave for town. She said, "I shall not depart from any place that God has given me. My property and my land by all rights belong to me and my children, and the Tatars shall not take them from me as long as God is my protector. I long ago entrusted myself to Him." Thus he was unable to convince her to leave and she remained in the village. Meanwhile, she began preparing to receive the guests, however unwelcome they may have been. She ordered [the peasants] to brew as much beer as possible. We also had our own wine, a blend of various types. And so in exactly two weeks, two hundred Bashkirs[17] came, all on horseback. The elders, accompanied by fifty of their ranks, came directly into the courtyard. My mother called upon God to assist her. She took us by the hand and went out to meet them on the porch. She greeted them as warmly as she could.

It was summertime, and they did not want to come indoors.

So my mother had all of them sit on carpets in the courtyard and ordered barrels of beer, wine, and liqueurs to be brought out, and she ordered a dinner to be prepared. After a while she commenced speaking with the leader about why they would want to offend her, a widow with small children. "I have no other protector except God, whom you know as well. He alone is our father. He created both me and you, so don't you fear His authority? Whither would you drive me from my land? I shall stay here alongside you and devote myself to serving you. Among you, too, are those who love God, and I can live serenely anywhere. People who are my peers do not frighten me, I hold everyone dear to me." She took us by the hand and said, "The fate of these orphans[18] lies in your hands. Do you wish to make them happy or unhappy?"

They began to speak among themselves, but my mother could not make out what they were saying. By then dinner was ready. My mother began to serve them herself, and she said, "I am serving you as if you were my friends and close neighbors. Partake of the bread and salt[19] of a widow, who is ever prepared to be a friend to you." By the end of dinner the leader and all of his subordinates stood up and went over to my mother and with tears in their eyes said, "Be at ease, our kind neighbor and friend, now we are not your enemies, but your protectors. All our strength is at your service, when something causes you fright or uneasiness, demand from us what you wish." My mother approached the leader, embraced him, cried, and then said, "I require nothing but your friendship and your kind hearts." They all shouted out in one voice and opened their hearts, "Behold, they are here!" And so, having spent the entire day feasting, they departed when it was already night. From that time on my mother lived amicably with them, and, on their side, they did her every possible kindness. On every holiday they came as guests to her house and they brought her gifts and invited her to visit them, especially for weddings. And my mother never turned them down.

One evening that summer a steward[20] showed up and said that someone had come to the village and was asking to spend the night, but he seemed somewhat suspicious. At that very same time two notorious atamans[21] were traveling around nearby with their party and they were plundering villages and burning them down. The last village they had burned lay just twelve versts away from us. But my mother was afraid of nothing and she remained very calm. When she heard the steward's report she ordered that the peasant be summoned to her, and he came. My mother asked, "Where are you from, my friend, and where are you headed?"

"To town, from the Demidov factory,"[22] he responded, "but I'm running late, and so I request that I may stay the night."

My mother said, "Spend the night, my friend, my peasants' huts are all empty, the masters are all out at work, so they cannot feed a man in transit as they ought to."

She summoned my nanny and said, "This is your guest, Kostentinovna.[23] Allow him to eat and drink, as God has sent him here, and then give him a place to sleep. Do you drink vodka, my friend?" And he said, "I do." My mother then got up and brought him some vodka.

And so he went off with nanny to her room. They fed him and put him to bed, and nanny suggested to him that he go to sleep. He said, "I will take a stroll for an hour and then I'll come."

When he had left nanny came and said, "Dear mother, enough. Is this a good man whom you have let stay the night? He has gone out somewhere."

My mother said, "He does seem suspicious to me, but what can I do about it? If I had not let him in it would have been worse. Pray to God, my friend. He will protect us. He once saved us from two hundred men, so He will truly save us from one." After a while our guest returned and went to sleep. My mother slept very little at night, but she lay down so that we would not be aware of her suspicions. In the morning the peasant came by to thank us for the bread and salt and for his time there, and he requested that he be allowed to leave. My mother answered, "May the Lord direct your path, and I will never refuse to serve you as well as I can." So he went off, and the servants gave him what he needed for the road.

In the winter we came into town and heard that both of the atamans had been captured. Since my mother often went to the prison, upon leaving the village she went straightaway to visit her friends—this is how she referred to them—and had us bring them everything a convict would need. We went into the prison and saw a man who knelt down and thanked us for the bread and salt. My mother recognized him as the one who had spent the night with us, and she asked him with surprise how he had ended up there. He answered, "Because of my own deeds. I am an ataman. When I went to your house I was afraid that another party might pillage you, so I protected you. Without you there would be no one to comfort the convicts. So that night I went out to the road by which I knew the party of another comrade would be coming. And I was not mistaken. I sent them off to a different place just to protect you. Indeed, do not fear any more, dear provider for the unfortunate. So long as you live even the bandits and evildoers will spare and protect you."

My mother came home and made an offering of thanks to God for His mercy, and she told me, "Never forget what happened here, my friend, and understand that good deeds are rewarded not only in the next life but even in this one. My daughter, do good works and take pleasure in doing kind deeds. Avoid all forms of vice and guard your heart against forbidden love. And when God blesses you with a husband, then respect your husband as your master, obey him, and love him with all your heart, even if he acts badly toward you. Know too that he was given to you by the Lord: the good for making you happy, and the bad to test your tolerance. If you bear all of this with humility, then you will have submitted to the will of God and not humanity. Never be so brazen as to reproach your husband, for this can lead only to discord between you. Meekness will have a greater effect than obstinacy on any evildoer."

And then my mother began to experience various illnesses and frequent attacks, and it became apparent that she was nearing the grave. And finally she could move about only when absolutely necessary, and this really frightened me, it was a terrible loss for me. At that very time Alexander Matveevich arrived,[24] and since he had been raised by my father, he dutifully paid his respects to my mother on the first day of his arrival. And my mother was very pleased to see him after sixteen years. And he asked her to introduce him to us, and I was summoned along with my little brother, and we were presented to him. And upon seeing him, I grew quite timid so that my legs trembled beneath me. And I was very glad when I was allowed to go to my room. He stayed a while, then left, and requested permission to visit often. His honored mother had been my mother's dear friend, and she had always wished to have me marry her son. When he got home he told his mother that he would be happy to have my hand in marriage. When she heard this she was overjoyed, and she said that she would like nothing more than to have me as her daughter. In the meantime he instructed his young niece to ask me whether I would be happy to marry him, and whether I found him in any way displeasing.

She came to our house on the third day of his stay and, finding a time when we were alone, she began to speak about him and to praise him to me. I responded that I was surprised that she had undertaken such a mission since she was herself a young woman. "And how could you think that I would answer you without my mother's knowledge? I don't undertake anything in this world without her. But if the Lord were to take her from me, then I would still have a friend in my nanny, without whom I cannot do anything. Or are you trying to take advantage of my youth and inexperience? You should know that I have been given rules of behavior, and I will never swerve from them. You extol his virtues, but I don't know whether you can come to know a person in three days. It may be that it is in your interest to speak to me thus, to deceive me like a child. However, I will tell you that I am not of an age to consider such a thing.[25] Above all, my mother is lying sick in bed, and my heart is full of sorrow. Even if I were of age, I would not allow myself to think of marriage. And so I beg you to say no more to me, and my nanny will know of this conversation. I will not mention it to my mother lest it worry her and exacerbate her illness."

Finally she began to beg me not to tell anyone, but I said to her firmly that I was not in the habit of keeping secrets from those who raised me. And so she departed. Once she had left I recounted the entire conversation to my nanny who embraced me and said, "My dear one, always remain this sincere and never conceal anything in your heart. The next time she comes to visit you, try not to be alone with her so that she does not have an opportunity to tell you any of her nonsense. Now you see the reason why we have not allowed you to choose your own acquaintances, and why your mother so rarely took you out visiting and lived with you in the village: to improve your heart and protect it from all misfortune. Learn and be wary in your choice of friends even after you are married. Never think that as a grown woman you are exempt from obeying those rules that you observed in childhood. They will be of use to you all your life and will protect you from a great deal."

After this I embraced my nanny, went up to my mother, and sat by her bed. As I gazed upon her, I felt a powerful trembling in my heart and began to weep bitterly, thinking that my mother was asleep. But she saw my tears and reached out her hand, which I kissed and bathed with my tears as she said to me, "My friend, I feel your love for me, and I know how bitter it is for you to part from me. But every life must come to an end. I will not deceive you. I feel my strength ebbing and I am nearing the grave."

I began to sob and I laid my head on her breast. She held me and soothed me, but she was so resolute that I didn't see any grief on her own face. Once again, she began to talk. "Do you not place your hope in the One who created you and has protected you to this day? He is your father, mother, protector, and friend. He will not leave you, but you must not forget Him, and you must hasten to Him whenever you are in need. You have yet another true friend, your nanny, who loves you, and neither you nor I should have any doubt about this. Simply be open with her and do not do anything without consulting her. You still have uncles and aunts, whom you must love and respect. Do not live with them, however, even if they invite you. Continue to do your exercises and do not disrupt your habitual routine. Remember your mother, who loved you and taught you to be a good Christian. Do not forget the prison and the poor, and go there in my stead so that they will not feel any loss. Then truly God will rain blessings upon you."

She lay silent for a bit and then she said, "Passion Week[26] is approaching. Go with nanny to the larder and prepare what is required for the convicts."

I went and told nanny my mother's orders. The two of us went to the larder and spent the entire day preparing things. Once we had gotten everything ready I again went to her and found Alexander Matveevich with her along with his mother, who came up to me and embraced me, and then asked, "Are you well? Why are your eyes red?" I could not utter a thing and simply pointed to my mother. She too started crying, and she said "God is merciful, my dearest child, be calm. You have friends who love you."

"But I will not have a mother," I said, "and what friends can take her place?" After this a general conversation ensued. They dined with us and spent the entire day.

I dearly wanted to go back to my own room: I was feeling some sort of anxiety combined with fear, but there was no way to leave my mother, to whom I had to administer medicine and nourishment. My brother came home from school, and Alexander Matveevich was very affectionate toward him. [My brother] was himself an affectionate type and my love for him was boundless. I liked to see him treated with affection. After that Alexander Matveevich visited us every day, but I disliked his visits, though I myself did not know why.

Passion Week arrived, and on Friday evening I went to the prisons with my nanny, and behind us the horses bore all the wares that we were to hand out. Everything was twice its normal quantity. It was as if my mother had foreseen that this was to be the last time that we would do this. We entered the prison quickly, and then all those unfortunate people began to weep and to ask whether my mother was still alive and whether there was any hope for her recovery. I too was weeping, and I told them that my mother was in danger. "Pray, my friends, that God will save her." They all grew silent and bowed their heads. One said with a groan, "God Our Lord, do You truly want to take her away from us and leave us orphans without any help?" And turning to me he asked, "Kind child, will you be like your mother and not abandon us when she is gone?" With tears in my eyes I said that I would respect her instructions and her will as if it were the law, and I would come to visit them with my friend as my mother had. They all said, "God bless you and grant you happiness now and forever."

Easter Sunday arrived and my mother appeared to be somewhat stronger. All the relatives had dinner at our house, and Alexander Matveevich said, "Treat me as family and allow me to spend the day with you."

All of Holy Week passed grimly in contemplation of my mother's illness; I never left her side, and I read to her from Scripture.[27] At night I lay beside her bed, but even sleep eluded me. When I would fall asleep, horrible dreams disturbed me, and I would awaken once more. In the week after Easter his sister arrived and asked to have a word with mama. After I had gone out she conveyed Alexander Matveevich's proposal to be accepted as a son.[28] My mother demurred due to my youth, but his sister said that my youth would be protected from everything, "She will have another mother who will love her and will keep her according to the rules she has been given." Knowing that he [sic] did not have long to live, the thought of being separated from me frightened my mother even more. So on that day she didn't say anything decisive.

Left by herself, she called to my nanny who stayed with her for some time. When she finally emerged she was all in tears. Seeing her in this state, I threw myself upon her and asked, "I can see that we are going to lose her; do you, too, honestly think that she is at death's door?"

My nanny simply said, "Pray, dear mother, and ask God for His mercy."

I again went to see my mother, who appeared upset. And she gave an order to send for my uncle and aunt, and when they arrived she spoke with them for a long time. My heart was pounding, I didn't know why, and I was saddened by all these secret negotiations. I had no idea what any of this meant. When the conversation was over my aunt and uncle emerged in tears. All of this surprised and frightened me, but out of respect I did not make so bold as to ask anything.

And so the matter was resolved without me. Alexander Matveevich got word of it three days later, but no one said anything to me. And it was resolved that we would go to the village, and on the way he was obliged to go around to the mines. When he had finished those visits he was to stay with us in the countryside to complete the arrangements. Within a week we took my mother to the village in such a weakened state that I thought she wouldn't make it. So many times I pleaded with my mother not to go but to stay in town for treatment, but without success. Once we arrived at the village various preparations were set in motion, and in response to my question as to why all this was taking place they responded that guests were arriving from Cheliaba. And so passed half of April.

~ II ~

May [1772] arrived, and on the thirteenth Alexander Matveevich and his mother and relatives arrived. They stayed with my uncle, and on that day he dined with us. On the morning of the following day my mother summoned me and began to speak, "My friend! Listen calmly to everything I am about to tell you. You see that I am so ill that there is no hope for my recovery, and even the doctor has said so. I do not fear death, and I hope for the mercy of my Savior, but it is bitter for me to leave you at this age. Now, though, you have another mother and another guardian, and you must not refuse to recognize them as such. By giving your consent you can extend my life a bit, and you will allow me to die in peace."

I had no suspicion that this had to do with my getting married, and I responded with tears that I had never violated her will, and I had always considered it a law that I should obey her. Could she really doubt that?

"Well, you should know that I have engaged you to Alexander Matveevich, and soon you will be his wife."

I was so dumbfounded that I was unable to utter a word,

and mother feared that there would be bad consequences. Finally I said, "Who will look after you?"

"They will not separate you from me," she answered, "and you will live with me."

"If that is so then let your will be carried out. I will obey you in all matters, but I am young and will not know how to please them."

"Certainly your youth frightens me, and if I did not see my own death nearing I would not have dreamt of giving you up.[29] But your obedience will bring you happiness, and your character will win their love. You know his mother; she loves you, and it remains for you merely to obey her and to do nothing without her counsel. I am quite certain that you will willingly carry this out without it's being a burden."

As I listened to what my mother was saying, my spirits sank. When she saw how burdened I was she stopped talking, embraced me, wept, and said, "Necessity forces me to do this. Be at ease and know that nothing happens without God's will."

I left her with a heavy heart. I had no tears but just a weight in my chest, and this sense of burden continued until the very day when my fate was sealed. However, could I have any idea as yet what a huge step this was toward a new life for me? I was thirteen years old. I had only one fear, that my esteemed mother would be taken from me, and I saw nothing else and thought of nothing else.

The wedding was set for the twenty-first of May. At that time I saw that all my relatives were acting despondently, and my friend—nanny—was in sorrow and tears every day, and this really upset me, but I did not think that she would be separated from me. So my intended husband's attentions became more open, but they did not make me joyful. I responded very coolly to them, and spent most of the time with my mother. My heart felt neither affection nor disgust, but mainly fear. Seeing this, he asked several times whether I was giving myself to him willingly, and was he in some way offensive to me? My response was, "I am carrying out my mother's will," and I ran away so that I would not be with him without others being present.

At last the day appointed for our wedding arrived. Early in the morning my mother sat me down and began to speak. "Now, my friend, this is the day on which you begin a completely new life, one you know nothing about. You will no longer be dependent upon me, but upon your husband and your mother-in-law, to whom you owe unbounded obedience and true love. You will no longer take orders from me, but from them. My authority over you has come to an end, and what remains is love alone and friendly advice. Love your husband with a pure and fervent love, obey him in everything; you will not be submitting to him but to God, for God has given him to you and made him your master. If he is cruel to you, then you will bear it all patiently and oblige him. Don't complain to anyone. People will not come to your assistance, and all you will do is expose his weaknesses, and bring dishonor on him and yourself.

"Always conduct yourself in such a manner that your conscience will be forever clear. Do not favor another man over him, even if he wears a crown.[30] Do not pay any attention to the flirtations of men, they are never sincere. He who loves you directly will not attempt to flatter. Conduct yourself so that no man would be so bold as to say something indecent to you, and do not have any close contact with any man of whom your husband does not approve. But be careful about this too. In your choice of friends don't rely on yourself, but defer to the choices of your new mother, who, out of her love for her son and for you, will provide you with kind and worldly friends from whom you will learn. Hide nothing from her that is in your heart, and in that way you will be spared many misfortunes that might otherwise befall you. Don't even conceal what other people say to you, for through this she will know those people and be able to tell you who is worthy of your friendship and who is not. This sincerity of yours will spare you from a great deal. If, in your youthfulness, you commit some indiscretion, don't be ashamed to reveal it, for in revealing it you avoid doing it again. Love your husband's mother, for she is your own. She is another me. Will you promise me, as your friend, that you will do all of this?"

I threw myself at her knees and wept, "I will do exactly as you say, even if they become my enemies and tormentors."

"I will say nothing about your brother. Your love will not leave him, and you will be a mother and gentle friend, and he too loves you and will heed you. If you end up living in high society, then in all of your pleasures do not forget to provide help for the poor and unfortunate. Do not become idle, for idleness is the mother of vice. Flee from pridefulness, be affectionate and indulgent toward all. Keep away from circumstances that might cause you to quarrel with anyone. In my entire life I never had enemies and never quarreled with anyone." After saying this she embraced me and blessed me, beseeching the Heavenly Father to help strengthen me and fortify my patience and goodwill. She foresaw that I would have to endure a great deal. And so, on this twenty-first day of May my fate was sealed.

We stayed in the countryside for a week after the wedding, but my mother's illness got worse, and we had to take her to town, not a great distance, only about ninety versts away. She was so weak, however, that every little movement caused her great suffering. Here is where my first source of grief began, when my husband refused to let me sit with her in the carriage. I obeyed him with grief-stricken tears, but without uttering a word. This journey was sheer torture for me; all gladness inside me died, and I felt nothing except a profound grief, and my thoughts were constantly with the sick one. Who is comforting her now? She is used to me, and I have eased her pain. This cruel man is depriving her of her only remaining comfort in her final days. Those were my very thoughts. In these depths only tears eased the burden.

My husband became enraged over my tears and he said to me, "From now on your love should be all mine, and you should give no thought to anything but how to please me. You now live for me and for no others."

"What could possibly diminish my love for her who is more precious to me than anything else in the world?" I asked. "Do you love your mother any less now that you are married? I'll do anything in the world for you, except this!"

He answered me, "You still don't understand the great obligations that you have toward a husband. So I will teach you!" And he said this in a voice that made my heart stop with fear. I grew silent, but I could not stop crying.

His favorite niece was sitting with us, and she laughed at my grief, saying to him, "I'm amazed that you don't make her stop. I'm tired of seeing these useless tears!"

He said, "Just you wait, my friend, there's still time. I don't want to start anything while we're on the road."

What was I to expect after these words? But I vowed in my heart not to say anything, and not to complain. Even more, I didn't want my mother to witness my grief. At last we arrived at the first station. I leapt out of the carriage to see whether my mother was still alive. I found her in such a weakened state that she couldn't speak or even give me her hand. I gave her some wine to drink and rubbed her with some vinegar, after which she got a bit stronger and asked me, "Are you well, my friend? Isn't your face unusually pale?"

"I am well, but your illness frightens me."

"What are you so scared of? Of course, I feel that I am rapidly approaching eternity."

I saw that we must not move her without letting her rest. I asked to be permitted to spend the night in the station, but my husband said to me, "You are not spending the night here. You're coming with me." I begged mightily to be allowed the pleasure of being at my mother's side. "At least I'll be able to see how she is doing and whether she can be moved."

He answered, "Others will do all of that without you."

I went to see my mother-in-law, who, upon seeing my pallid complexion and my swollen eyes, embraced me and asked, "What has happened to you?" I responded that we were leaving at once, and my sick mother was being left behind, and I was afraid that she might die.

I then fell to my knees, "Do me this first kindness. Stay with her and I will be much more at ease!" She began to weep and said that even had I not asked she would not have left her by herself, and she would keep her as peaceful as she could. My nanny was not with us since she had been sent ahead to town to make the necessary preparations for us. So we went to town, leaving mother behind. I thought I would never see her again, and I barely remember how the trip ended. We arrived in town around suppertime. Nanny met us and prepared supper. I couldn't eat a thing, and all I did was cry. My bitter tears caused my niece more laughter than sympathy, which is what she should have felt. You see, my mother had been her benefactress.

After supper we went to bed. [The niece] began to take her leave of her uncle and then she started to weep. He grew alarmed and said to her, "Why are you so distressed, my dear one? I know that your love for me is so great that it's hard to bear even one night without seeing me. Whereas my wife would gladly have stayed with her mother: that's how differently the two of you behave, so I will not let you sleep anywhere except in our bedroom."

I was silent, but my nanny began to sob and she left the room saying, "This is my angel's fate!"

My husband was extremely angered and he said to me, "You shall no longer have any connections with her and I forbid you to speak with her, and she must never be in your company again!"

And his niece said to him, "I fear that she might tell your mama, so wouldn't it be better just to send her to the country right now?"

I then said that this was out of the question since she was the only one who could be with my ill mother. I understood that I could be with her only at prescribed times, so it was simply unthinkable to remove the dying woman's last comfort. "Now, regarding what you are afraid of, that she will speak, let me set your minds at rest. She will never speak to anyone. But I find it hard to understand what you are afraid of when you love your uncle. I love my uncles too and I do not fear letting the whole world know about my affection." I said all this sincerely and with a good heart, not knowing about the vices of love. And so we went to bed.

My nanny wanted to come in to help me undress, but they told her that I no longer required either her services or her counsel, and that she should not make so bold as to enter where she was forbidden. Here was yet another woe for my already burdened heart! I asked, "For God's sake, tell me how she has angered you so that you behave so harshly toward her? I had harbored the hope that you would be grateful to her for having raised me. Obviously I have been deceived in all of this! They told me that a husband would love me no less than my mother does and would care for me, but I do not know what kind of strange love this is. Tell me, do you love me?" He then asked me the same thing.

"I would love you if you did not take from me that which is most precious to me in the world and did not separate me from those who are dearest to me. Let me ask you what you would do in my place if you were treated as harshly as I have been?" After saying this I cried bitterly and rushed to embrace him, "Do not torment me! You were given to me in order to ease my woes and love me, and in return I will give you love, respect, and obedience."

He was touched by this and said, "I do love you."

"If you love me. then give me your word that you will not forbid me to be with my mother and nanny. I will not say anything to them that you don't want. You will tell me what to say and what not to say. I promise never to be alone with them, and your mother will always be present, and she will hear my conversations and see what I do. I would sooner open my heart to her now than to my own mother: I was told that she would take the place of my friends."

He gazed at me intently and said, "You shouldn't discuss everything, not even with my mother. I don't want her to know everything that happens in your heart and that takes place between us."

I was utterly dumbfounded and remained silent for some time. Even my tears stopped, and my breathing became very labored. He grew frightened and rushed out to get me some water. Nanny saw that he was distressed and asked what was going on. He simply cried out, "Water!"

She poured some water and rushed over to me and said, "Now no one will hold me back!" When she came to me and saw how pale and weepy I was, she shook me and made me drink the water. Even water was too much for me, and I was unable to swallow. She threw herself on her knees before my husband and requested that he not send her away from me, "You still don't know her and her moods. She'll die!"

There was nothing for him to do! He said, "Look after her and help her. I am unable to be with her since I am not in the best shape myself." And he left with his niece for another bedroom that had been made ready for my mother.

She sat by me and asked what had happened to me. I looked at her and said, "You taught me to be sincere and not to conceal anything that is in my heart. You also told me to love my husband and to obey him in everything and to carry out his wishes. So I will ask of you now: is this truly my obligation?" She said to me, "Without love and obedience a person cannot be happy, and this is especially true with respect to a husband."

"But about sincerity, what do you say?"

"It too is necessary, but you must be circumspect about whom you are sincere to. Don't be so with everyone."

"Whom do you name for me, and with whom should I be frank?"

"To your husband and no one else, and also to his mother, who truly loves you, and she will offer you good and useful advice."

"Apparently I am now completely in a different school. My first lessons brought gladness and contentment to my heart, but these bring grief and dejection. Still, you have taught me to be tolerant and silent, and this latter lesson will now be the most useful. You are my friend, and I love and honor you a great deal, but do not ask anything more of me." She wept and asked me to lie down, but I said, "I am unable to sleep, and I do not wish to."

I went off to find out whether my husband had calmed down, and I found him sleeping together with his niece on one bed embracing one another. My obedience and ignorance were so great that this did not affect me, and I did not even keep it secret. When I came up to my nanny she asked me,

"So, mother dear, how is he?" I said, "Thank God, he is sleeping very peacefully with Vera Alekseevna,[31] and she is holding him in a friendly manner." Nanny looked at me very intently and, seeing my utter calm, kept silent, but she sighed heavily. I sat by the window, thinking—what, I didn't know myself: I did wonder about my mother, whether she was alive, but took comfort knowing she was not alone.

At that time the sun began to rise, and I recalled the peaceful times when I sat by the shore with my mother or my nanny, and the great contentment I felt at that time. I compared that with my current, tormented state. Tears welled up involuntarily, and I said, "I do not know if you did the best thing when you gave me a husband and took me away from my happy life and made me feel such grief so soon."

She looked at me and said, "Be at ease, my inestimable one, and recall: isn't there a God who pays attention to the prayers of a pure and obedient heart? Entrust all your sorrows to Him, for He is your solace. He will provide the strength and fortitude for bearing all unpleasantness. Just have faith, hope, and love for Him. He never abandons those who love Him. That should be enough comfort for your heart, do not complain about us. We never wished you misfortune. Were it possible, I would buy you good fortune with my own life. Today toward evening your mother will be here. Try as best you can to calm yourself so that she does not see your grief. You might speed up her death and bring it nearer."

At that moment my husband walked in. I went up to greet him, and I asked if he was well and how did he sleep? He asked me, "And how are you? Did you drink some tea?"

"I don't drink tea, but they will give me some milk."

Nanny went off to make tea, and he sat next to me. I wanted to show him that I was interested in him, and with a cheerful face I said, "I went over to see if you were sleeping soundly and I found you pleasantly asleep with Vera Alekseevna: and so, in order not to waken you, I left for the bedroom." And suddenly I glanced over at him: he had turned completely pale. I asked what had happened to him. He was silent for a long while and finally he asked whether I came to him by myself or was I with nanny? I said, "Alone," and he became extremely affectionate with me, and looked me straight in the eye. I was so embarrassed that I could not raise my eyes to him.

Then he said, "I do not know whether you're being cunning or simply naive."

I looked at him and began to weep. "How can you think this way about me? When have I ever been deceitful with you? That's really not something I am schooled in, but I say what I think." I really did not understand what he was talking about.

After a while tea appeared. I began to serve it and had his niece summoned. She came and I greeted her with affection. I then left them to go and get dressed. Nanny said to me, "Don't tell your husband that you went to their room during the night."

"Why not?" I asked, surprised. "I can't keep anything from him. In fact, I already told him."

"You didn't say that I know, did you?"

"No!"

"Then I beg you not to, if you love me."

I looked at her and said, "My God, how you all torment me! Now I don't know what to do. There must be something or other that you don't want to say to me, and I don't understand anything, and I never will! All right, I will promise you and I will not tell him that you know. But I beg you as a friend: explain to me this strange and tiresome life I now lead. Before marrying me off you should first have taught me how to live with a husband. You have brought me to this point in such a short time that I don't know what I am and what to do!"

She cried and said, "Whom are you blaming? Your mother? She who loves you so much and who spared nothing on your behalf? Are there any people who can foretell what will happen to them? Oh, if the lot of everyone were known in advance, then no one would be unhappy! But every person must be prepared to bear any cross and to bear all that is necessary with humility. It is impossible to have everything be sweet, one must also taste the bitter. Be steadfast. God will not abandon you."

And so the day passed. Evening fell and they brought my mother in her terribly weakened state, carried her into the room, and put her down on a bed that had been prepared for her. The doctor was already there with me awaiting her, and after he gave her medication she perked up a bit and my heart became calmer because I was with her. From that moment all my time was devoted to caring for my ill mother. I asked my kind mother-in-law to request of my husband that he permit me to be with my mother and that he not be angry with me on account of my love for her.

She asked me, "Does he really forbid you, my friend?" I answered with tears. She embraced me and said, " Be calm and love me, and be pure-hearted with me. I will supply you with all the joys that I can."

Day by day my mother grew worse and it was evident that death was nearing. During the last week of her life I did not leave her side; day and night I stayed by her. On the eve of her death, early in the morning, she looked at me and said, "How you have changed, my friend. It is unpardonable for you to kill yourself this way. Long ago you were prepared for an eternal separation from me. I didn't conceal from you the fact that my days were numbered and that this very fact obliged me to give you away in marriage. I do not know how your life will be, but however it may be, don't blame me, my dearest!"

I threw myself down to kiss her hands, and just sobbed.

"It seems to me that your husband has a passionate nature, and perhaps there is something else about him that I did not notice before. But the deed is done. My only hope is in my friend, his mother; and I asked her and am sure that she alone can provide support for you and for your tender youth. Just be virtuous, obedient, and patient. Bear everything without reproaching the mercy of Our Father. My love for you is great, but it cannot compare with His. If out of my own love I did not refuse you anything, could He refuse you His mercy? Just love Him and be obedient in all things. Oh, my dear friend! You must also love your husband and bear his weaknesses . . . I cannot say any more, my spirit is spent . . . ."

I said to her, "Be content, I will be happy." She was quiet a while and then said, "Kostentinovna will not go with you, because your husband does not want to have her around, and you will not oppose his wish." I took a deep breath and said, "My God! And now my last friend is being taken from me! And so I will be all alone in the world, without help and without advice! Oh, mother! Did you ever think that I would be left all by myself, so young and inexperienced? But be content, dear mother, even alone I shall live by your precepts and I shall not forget those rules which you gave me."

She had grown so weak and sad that she was unable even to cry. My mother-in-law came in, and my mother grabbed me by the hand, gave it to her and said simply, "I am handing her over to God and to you. Be her friend and the guardian of her youth!"

My husband came in rarely, pleading that he was busy with his own affairs. In the evening [mother] told nanny to send word to the churchman that after early vespers[32] he should give her confession and administer the sacraments.

She [nanny] asked, "Do you really feel something?"

She answered, "Of course, my friend. I will very soon be leaving you."

Nanny began to weep. My mother looked at her and said, "Don't cry! All your service, love, and friendship will bring you comfort."

"How can I take comfort," she answered, "after having lost the one who was not a mistress to me, but a mother, and who valued my small services and honored me with the name of 'friend'? Where else will I find that goodness which is being taken from me for eternity? My very soul will not be contented until I die. If only I could be consoled by being useful to the daughter you are leaving! I would go to the ends of the earth for her, I would abandon my husband and children, but even this is denied me!"

She responded, "You cannot [stay with her], much as I would have have wished it. Now it is too late to repair the damage, we can only leave it to God: He alone can correct everything." Right then my husband came in and told nanny to leave with her stupid tears. My mother said, "Don't touch her, my friend, and forgive her: she is being separated from two friends: from one eternally, and from the other temporarily, but probably for a long time. No one can enter into her grief except me. These tears are not flattery—I know her and I value her friendship and service a great deal. Let her stay with me while I am still alive. I also request that after I am gone you also do everything possible to make her content, and I beseech you not to make her sad, and let her live just a little longer with the young ones. This will lighten her burden and bring peace to my remains."

My husband was very displeased by this, but he promised to carry out her wishes and he left the room. In the evening he had me summoned to supper. I went and sat at the table, but I couldn't eat a thing. Once I was done I approached my husband to excuse myself, and he told me, "Soon you will lose your mother, she is in a bad way, but your tears, which I find unbearable, will cease that much sooner."

I went to my ill mother and sat down. My mother-in-law had not left her. Throughout the night she said very little and she seemed to be more or less sleeping, only from time to time she said her prayers. Morning arrived and at six o'clock the priest came, confessed her, administered the sacraments, and administered the last rites. After this my mother was at peace, but she requested that he return to her as soon as possible. When he did come she requested that he read her the prayer for the departing, and she had herself seated and the crucifix placed in front of her, and she asked my mother-in-law to take me away and to put me somewhere where she could not see me. When she had finished all of this, she summoned my brother and me to her. She kissed us and blessed us. She kissed my mother-in-law and nanny, and she summoned all the rest. She blessed all of them for their faithfulness and their attentiveness. After all of this, she lay down and began to pray, and she could no longer look at anything except the crucifix.

It was ten o'clock in the morning on the twenty-first of July [1772]. She crossed herself three times and said something indecipherable, took a breath, and that breath was her last. There was no regret on her face. I looked at her and could not quite imagine that I had lost her so soon, but my mother-in-law approached me, embraced me, grabbed me by the hand

and said, "So, my friend, it's all over: she is no more!" I tore myself away and threw myself on the body, spilled tears on its face and hands, called out to her . . . And then they led me away from the body and brought me to another room. I didn't know what I was or where I was. The tears had stopped, and I developed a bad fever, and by nightfall I was hot and delirious.

By the morning of the next day I had regained my senses and my first words were, "Where is my remaining friend?" My mother-in-law said that she would be there immediately, and there she was. There was such grief on her face that I could not look at her. I gave her my hand, saying only, "She has left us, it is all over!" And then my tears returned and eased my suffering heart, and I requested that my mother-in-law let me go to the body.

My husband entered and said not to let me, but his mother told him, "It is not possible that she not be by the side of her mother's body! Enter into her grief: she has lost everything. She had a rare mother, permit her to ease her grief by remaining with the body. Leave her, my friend, under my care. Of course, I will protect her, and you can be sure that she is very dear to me. This is a trust given to me in friendship, and now my life is joined with her life, and her contentment is my own contentment. The deceased—my friend and benefactress—for me is still alive in her daughter and her son, who also is dear to me."

At this point they brought my brother to me. He rushed to embrace me, and with bitter tears he asked, "Are you ill? Will you abandon me just as mama did?"

I stood up for his sake, although I supported myself on my legs with difficulty, and I said, "Don't cry, my friend, I am well. What you see is not illness but grief, which has obliged me to lie down in bed."

My husband took one look at everything and was greatly displeased, and he approached his mother and said, "Do whatever you wish, I am going off to ready the horses and to get everything we need to take the body to the country." My second mother did not leave me. She prevailed upon me to drink a cup of tea, and went with my brother and me to view the body. When we entered and I saw my mother's lifeless body I began to weep. I kissed her hand and sat by the table on which she lay. My entire future revealed itself to me at that moment in a most unhappy light, and I saw myself and my orphaned brother, alone without any help in the whole world. Who would comfort us, who would advise us, to whom should I turn? And with these mournful thoughts I sat in that one place the entire day, and no one could talk me into leaving.

By evening the beggars and the poor—those who had been the beneficiaries of her blessings—had gathered, and there was such a crush of people in the room that there was no space at all. There was so much lamenting it was awful. They had all spent the night sleeping outside her window, knowing that the body would be brought out in the morning. The next morning I received a note from the prison requesting that I ask the prison director for a final kindness on their [i.e., the convicts'] behalf: that they be permitted to pay their respects to the body of their mother. I went myself to see the director, a good man and fond of us. As soon as I entered his room he began to weep bitterly, and he expressed surprise that I would be there at this time. As soon as he learned the reason he said, "I will make the [funeral] procession of the body of our common mother and benefactress truly grand. I will be there myself at your house with the convicts, who are inconsolable at the loss of their benefactress."

When I arrived home they had already begun to ready the horses, and within two hours everything was prepared. They intoned the funeral service for my mother and began to carry her out, to put her on the hearse. They had only just opened the gates when a frightful noise, moaning, and clatter of chains began, and they all rushed to the coffin and fell on the ground and cried out: "Farewell, our nurturer and mother! You have left us, poor orphans! Oh, God! Accept our heartfelt prayers and comfort her soul!"

There was no room in the courtyard among the beggars and poor, and only with a great effort were they able to carry out the body in such a crush. This ceremony and clatter of chains continued for five versts. When the director stopped the procession and told them to say their last farewell, I can't describe the horrible weeping and shouting, which arose as if in a single voice. Many of them could not remain on their feet, and so they fell down. The director himself was in no condition to utter a word. My husband alighted from the carriage, went up to the director, and requested him to put an end to this scene as soon as possible. "Don't be surprised by this," responded the director. "And don't rush to tear these unfortunate souls away from the coffin of the one who called them her friends. They have lost everything that had brightened up their unfortunate life! Permit them to collect themselves, I will lead them away and give you peace. You will find it, but not they!"

I was sitting, or to be more precise, lying in the carriage. They threw themselves upon me, kissed my hands and feet and cried, "Daughter of our benefactress, do not leave us convicts while you remain here! But they'll take you, too, from us, and then there will be no one left who will ease our lot!"

With some difficulty I managed to raise myself up, and I said, "My friends, you will not be abandoned. I will give this order to the overseer. Even as she lay dying my mother thought about you. Kostentinovna will do everything that you need."

Two days prior to her death my mother had given me five hundred rubles for my own expenses, and I had them with me.[33] I took out three hundred and distributed it among them. They gave them over to the director and said, "You take them, father, for our needs."

"Let us say our farewells one last time!"

My mother-in-law told them, "Friends, be gentle with her, the surviving daughter, who has lost all her strength!"

And so we left and they cried out after us, "Protect the daughter our mother left behind! May God's blessing be with her!"

After forty versts the peasants[34] came out to meet the body; they stopped the horses and carried the coffin in their arms the rest of the way to the village. I gazed upon this ceremony with great despondency and grief! What despair I saw on the faces of those peasants! Some were sobbing, others were unable to sob, and only their hushed moaning was audible! Finally they placed the body in the grave, and for that entire day it was as if the whole village was empty. No one appeared on the streets, and the people merely went to church to pay their respects at the grave. On the third day the overseer, along with some peasants, came to my husband when his mother and I were with him. He threw himself at his feet, began to weep and said, "We entrust to you our mother's right to rule over us. Instruct us and order us what to do. We still have masters, but they are not of age. One is not here, the other is entrusted to you, so that our dear young mistress can bring him up. As they raised her so she will raise him."

My husband said that everything would remain the same as before. "I will leave a guardian behind to whom you should turn for everything." And they went out.

We stayed in the village for two weeks, and I would have liked to remain there for six, but my husband said, "Your aunt and uncle [who live here] will carry out the rites[35] without you." So they ordered the horses to be readied, so that we could leave the next day [August 1772], and I went to take leave of my uncle.

Upon seeing me all in tears, they realized that we would be going early on the following day. Auntie began to cry bitterly and she said,

"Go then, my kind friend. The Lord be with you! This will be your first time outside the excellent life of our quiet little refuge, but you will come to enjoy the delights of the city, to which you are not yet accustomed. But grow accustomed you must, dear one, and you must not become discontented. That husband of yours loves society, more as a kind of amusement, and you too must love it and live as he chooses. Do not get in the habit of gainsaying your husband, but rather do as he wishes. No husband will demand anything that you cannot do. Still one more word: your husband came to me yesterday and asked that your friend, Kostentinovna, stay here in some capacity. I have already told her, and she has agreed, albeit with sadness. I ask you to be reasonable about this and not to ask that she go with you.

"You must unfailingly and obediently submit to all experiences that your husband imposes upon you. By your own submission and obedience you shall win his love. I had better tell you that he let us know that it would be better for us to remain here. Apparently he wants to distance you from everything that can remind you of your mother. I see that this makes you sad, and I share in your grief, but, my friend, you should already be living under his laws. We have done the same for our husbands. You already know how great and sacred is your obligation to your husband, so, when you carry this out, you shall be carrying out God's law. Your main responsibility will consist in not undertaking anything he does not wish you to do.

"Your second obligation is to love and honor his mother and to solicit her counsel in everything, and to be true to her. She is good and wise and will give you those precepts that your own mother, may she rest in peace, gave you. Try as much as possible not to waste your time and not to engage in frivolities. If someone recommends some books for you to read, don't read them until your mother has looked them over. When she does recommend one to you, you can safely make use of it. Do not be friendly with his niece and do not open your heart to her. When she speaks with you, if she says something dubious or unpleasant, mention it quietly to his mother.

"Try to be affectionate and attentive toward all his family even though they may not reciprocate. Do not forcibly demand that your husband express love to your own family. Your own love for us is enough. Do not get annoyed if he complains about us in your presence. Let it go and don't come to our defense. My friend, trust that I have experience in everything that I am telling you. Follow those rules and conduct yourself in such a way that you will feel no pangs of conscience, and in that way you shall be beloved of God, who will protect you in all things and who will not abandon you. If you wish to know how we are, then inquire of your husband whether he will allow you to write to us, and once you've written a letter, show it to him or to your mother-in-law for their approval. If for some reason you are not allowed to write, then do not get upset: we will always be certain of your love toward us, and we will always have news of you. But you must not undertake to write us in secret, don't keep anything secret from your husband, better to ask your mother-in-law. She will know better what to do."

I listened to all of this, and finally I said, "What a burdensome set of responsibilities you lay out for me! Why didn't you tell me about any of this before my betrothal? What kind of law is this—get married and lose everything that you hold dear? And how can it be that I must not share my love with my family! Why then don't I forbid him from loving his? If he did not love those close to him I would think badly of him. This is what you've done to me: you have separated me from you! It would make things easier for me to leave you post haste! Let the physical remoteness separate us out of necessity, and we will not see each other! I shall carry out all of your instructions, but you cannot lift the burden in my heart. That is not in my power, nor in yours!"

My aunt stood up, embraced me, and said, "Now it is time for me to say farewell to you, my angel! May the Lord bless you with kindness and patience!"

My uncle could not utter a word, and he sat still the entire time with his head down. I glanced over at him and saw the tears flowing down his cheeks, and I threw myself upon him. "Don't cry for me. I will be happy, just pray for me!" He just held me close to him and overflowed with tears.

My aunt forcibly pulled me away from him and said, "Better to bless her than to have such a bitter parting." And so I left for home.

Instead of leaving in the morning as was normal, we set off at night when everyone was asleep, and no one saw our departure but my poor, sad nanny, who was more dead than alive as she parted with me, her face was terribly pale. She could no longer cry, and I saw that she was staggering and barely able to stand. Her eyes were dark and wild, and I had a deep dread that something most dire would happen. Her husband came up to me and said, "Pardon us, our kind and gentle soul! May God grant you as much good fortune as we wish for you! Let us go, wife, and let us not trouble her any more." A young shepherd boy ran toward us shouting, "Let me say farewell to

her! If you refuse I shall die!" My husband wasn't going to let
him, but my mother-in-law said, "It would be shameful to deprive her of this final pleasure. It pains me to see how indiffer-
ent you are to her suffering!"

At that point I glanced back and saw my poor nanny lying
unconscious in the middle of the courtyard. I cried out, "For
God's sake, let me embrace her one last time! I will return her
to life that way!" My mother-in-law approached her with me
and we revived her, but she was unable to speak. I kissed her
and said, "Take care of yourself for my sake." And I called over
the shepherd and asked him to go up to my uncle and wait
until my aunt awoke and tell her to take in the ill woman and
care for her, and protect her. They would be doing this not for
her but for me, and by this they would be showing their love
for me. I also told him to send a special messenger to let me
know about her condition.

Thus I left my peaceful enclave with a heart filled with
grief, and I've never been there since.

~ III ~

We arrived in town and the festivities commenced at our
house, but I was unable to take part. He brought his niece to
live with us. We were all together in the daytime, and at bed-
time his niece would come and go to bed with us. And if she
felt cramped, or for some other reasons that at that time I did
not understand, they would send me away to sleep on the
couch. Since I had not yet gotten over my sense of loss, I was
just as glad to be alone and able to think freely and get up
early, as was my habit, instead of lying in bed until eleven
o'clock as my husband usually required me to do. For me this
was torture, and I felt a deathly melancholy not to see the sunrise and to be required to lie in bed even though I was not
asleep. This way of life had weakened me to such an extent
that I had stopped sleeping and had lost my appetite. I had no

taste for anything, and I grew thin and wan, and I stayed this way for about four weeks.

My mother-in-law grieved over me and she too stopped sleeping, and one night she wanted to see whether I was sleeping. She came in very quietly and found me lying on the couch, and my husband with his niece. When she saw this she began to tremble and she went away immediately. The next day she came to me because a headache now kept me bedridden. And when she was alone with me, she asked why I was sleeping on the couch. I answered, "They told me that Vera Alekseevna didn't have enough room and I was disturbing her. So I'm letting her be comfortable, without thinking about myself." She started to cry and scolded me for my lack of candor in saying nothing to her before this. I answered that I considered it unimportant. "And I ask you, as my benefactress and mother, to leave me here when you all go to Petersburg. You don't need me there, and here I can still be useful to others. I assure you that I will not complain about your son, I will only blame myself for not knowing how to love and please a husband. What joy would it bring you to see someone you love in torment, who has done you no harm and could love your son if only he wished it? Do me this one kindness and take me away to the country so that I may die there among my friends! You, of course, will not refuse to be with me, as a final kindness. It is always very pleasant for me to see you, and I love you no less than my own mother. Recall that at the time of my mother's death I was handed over to you, and except for you, I have no one else in the world. My relatives and all my friends have been removed and taken from me!"

She cried bitterly and said, "My friend, why are you killing yourself in this way? God is merciful and he can fix everything! We shall pray and hope. It seems to me that your husband loves you. Otherwise why would he have married you? No one forced him!"

"This is a mysterious kind of love! Does everybody love in this way at the place where he wants to bring me,[36] and is this the kind of moral upbringing that they consider the best and most enlightened?

"Why did you take me away from my blissful circumstances and bring sorrow to my heart so early? You knew me well, and you knew that I lived among friends and I thrived on their love, and was merry. What will become of me now? Oh, how I wish to be united with my honored mother! There is only one other thing that keeps my heart beating, and that is love for my brother, who has no one but me. Look after him, kind mother, and at least don't let him feel that all is lost!"

She embraced me and said, "Be calm, my inestimable daughter and friend! You will find everything in me: I will share in everything with you." And on that day she did not leave me.

By the evening I had grown feverish and delirious, and they say that I raved on, calling upon my mother and all my friends to take me to them. My mother-in-law sat throughout the night in fear and even in desperation over me, but my husband went out to the mines. In the morning they summoned the staff doctor, who said that I had a severe and dangerous fever, and he doubted that I would survive it. My mother-in-law threw herself on her knees before him, "For God's sake save her; use all the means you have to heal her! You were a friend of her mother, and now you must know the cause of her illness: a powerful shock brought on by the loss of her mother and the separation from her friends."

I lay twenty days without hope! My mother-in-law sent for nanny in the country and asked for my aunt and uncle to come. I was surrounded by my friends and insensible to their grief! They confessed me and performed the Last Rites. On the twenty-first day I regained consciousness and what was the first thing I saw but my nanny, and I thought I was dreaming, and I lay back down and closed my eyes. The next day my hearing returned and I started to make sense of what people were saying. The doctor said that there now was hope that I would live. And I admit I was terribly sorry to hear this. I would have departed this world with pleasure. I also saw my husband sitting at my feet and weeping bitterly. This touched me so deeply that I gathered the strength to raise my hand and give it to him. He noticed my movement and came up to me.

I looked at him, took his hand, and clasped it to my heart. He fell on his knees and began to weep. My mother and family persuaded him not to revive my illness with his own grief. In this way I found out that all those dear to my heart were with me. I asked about my brother, whom they then brought to me at once. He embraced me and asked, "Now you won't die, and your Sasha will not be orphaned."

And so, my recovery proceeded very gradually. For two months I could not walk by myself. I was frightfully thin and jaundiced, and I had a severe cough. The doctor feared consumption,[37] but I improved slowly but surely, and by December [1772] I had completely recovered. During the entire time my husband rarely left my side, and his concern for me soothed me immensely. To the extent that I was able I tried to show him my feelings, by taking joy in his ministering and by expressing my gratitude. My contentment and total recovery gladdened my mother-in-law and all my family. My aunt and uncle went back to the country. My mother-in-law would not let my nanny go, and so nanny was quite happy to stay. One day I asked my mother-in-law, "Where is Vera Alekseevna?" She said, "Don't mention her to me. I do not want to see her!"

My contentment did not last for long, however. That evening I was sitting in my room, reading. My husband came over to me and was very affectionate, and then he asked, "Why are you angry at poor Vera Alekseevna?"

I told him that he had no reason to think I was angry with her. "I even asked your mother about her. She ordered me to be silent and not to mention her, saying 'I don't want to see her.' Why don't you ask her yourself how Vera Alekseevna made her so mad, but I don't even know how long it's been since she was here, or why."

My husband said, "At the very outset of your illness she was beaten and thrown out by my mother for no reason."

This surprised me tremendously. "Knowing the gentleness and kindheartedness of my mother-in-law, what you say greatly surprises me, and mother would not act so harshly without cause. But more than that she was her favorite granddaughter. You should endeavor to learn the reason and to force her to ask your mother's forgiveness." But he asked me to do it and to ask his mother to let his niece live with us until our departure. I said that I was not allowed to speak about her, and I didn't dare.

He looked at me very angrily and said, "I demand that you do this, otherwise you will receive no love or affection from me, and once again everything will be taken away from you. I shall go to her at once and spend a more pleasant night there than here. Do you think that I don't know what your game is?"

I started to cry and then answered that what he was saying had never entered my thoughts. "You told me yourself that she had been thrown out while I was ill, so how could I have had a part in this?" He left without saying a word.

My mother-in-law had been waiting a long time for us, and when she could wait no longer she came into my room. When she saw that I was alone and weeping, she began to ask questions. I recounted everything to her. She was about to get really mad, but I said, "What are you going to do? You'll only make me miserable again. After all, he'll keep going to go see her; even today he wanted to spend the night there. I don't know how you can improve the situation. People can gossip about his behavior, which will be hard on you. Oh, dear mother, why did you rush me into this misfortune before I learned about his character? To my misfortune I see that nothing is sacred to him. I fear that he will lose respect even for you. What can you do then? For now try to find ways to protect me as much as you can."

I truly do not know what happened or how, but in a few days Vera Alekseevna appeared and immediately came to live with us until our departure, and my life was all pure misery. My husband set his niece to watch over me so that I could not go anywhere or speak with anyone without her, lest I start to complain. But I had no such intentions. My mother-in-law insisted that she [Vera] be with us only during the day, and after supper she had to go off to her room at once. But even during the day when we sat alone, such abominations took place that were impossible to look upon still. I had to bear everything, nevertheless, because they wouldn't let me leave. Out of shame

I closed my eyes and cried when I saw all of this. Finally I even stopped crying. I made a firm decision to stop living with my husband and to stay in Siberia, but I remained silent until they started packing to leave.

Lent arrived, and as was my custom, I ordered that fish be prepared for me, and meat for my husband. But he told me that I had to eat what he ate without fail. I beseeched him and said that I simply could not, that it was strictly forbidden, and I considered it a sin. He began to laugh and said that it was foolish to think that anything was a sin. "It's high time you let go of all this foolishness, and I order you to eat."

He poured soup and gave it to me. Several times I raised the spoon toward my mouth, but my pounding heart and shaking hand prevented it from reaching my mouth. At last I began to eat, and I received affection and approval for this from my husband, but instead of soup I only ate tears. Throughout Lent I was distressed and my conscience tormented me. The time came when we had to prepare to travel, and this latest journey was to last six hundred versts to where his sister and brother-in-law lived, so that we could greet the holiday there and stay until the dry weather. His niece begged to go with us and beseeched him with tears, saying that she would die without him. He gave her his word that he would not part from her. My relatives all gathered when they learned that we would soon be departing.

One evening my husband was not home, and I went to my mother-in-law and said that they should not pack anything of mine. "Though it is difficult for me, I shall not go with you. I swear to you that I do not have strength to bear all these abominations! I am so young that I am afraid for myself, afraid that I'll start believing that there is no such thing as sin and that I may allow myself anything. What then will become of me? And how will it be for you to see the shame of your daughter and son? That could kill you. I am sure that he will display remorse over me, but don't believe it. Let him enjoy his perfect contentment! I assure you that I won't complain about him to anyone, and everyone will think that it's me, and blame it on my youth. I also know that you do not have an easy time of it and your income is small, so I will give you a letter of credit for Demidov,[38] from whom you will receive half of the 16,000 [rubles]. I cannot do any more for you, but you can bring me eternal peace and prove how much mercy you have for me by not opposing me in this, and by departing without rancor from one who will never cease loving you, honoring you, and calling you her dear mother.

"At the present time he [Karamyshev] can make good the promise that he gave to Vera Alekseevna that he would never be apart from her. Why would you want to torment me? I have done nothing but give you love and respect, but I ask you not to chide him for my sake, and thereby prove to me your final act of love. Let him think that I do not love him, as I confess to you I do not. Don't blame me for speaking with you so frankly. You yourself must agree that it is impossible to love such a man. Will you tell me that I can force myself to love? That is not possible. I won't try to flatter you in this way: no one can force love. Here, my honored mother, I have told you everything that was in my heart and I am deliberately saying this before all my family, so that my decision will be known to you."

They all remained dumbfounded, but my mother-in-law sat and remained silent and just wept. My uncle started to say that he disapproved of my actions, that I should remember my promise to my mother at the end of her life "that you will endure and bear everything."

"My friend, whose will you are resisting? God's! Can you tear asunder those sacred bonds by which you are joined for all time? Who gave you the right to choose your own fate? You have always been taught to deliver yourself to the will of our Savior, and in Him alone to seek your solace and the fortress of your strength. How can you know, once you have left your husband, whether you will be content and happy, and that your conscience will not begin to trouble you? And to what are you exposing your youth? To shame and censure, which you will bring down on your family as well. You will be disturbing your parents in their graves. Do you think that they will not suffer, seeing you throw off all of the responsibilities of marriage? That alone should be horrible for you, and God's judgment will fall upon you. Do you really think that you are the only one in this world who suffers so much? Believe me, my dearest, there are marriages far worse and more unfortunate than yours, and there are wives who are left entirely alone, without friends, without support, but our Maker is still merciful to you. He gave you a sincere friend in your mother-in-law, and yet you still complain!" My mother suddenly threw herself on her knees before me. "I implore you on the grave of your mother and my grief: do not send me to my grave in torment! I assure you that Vera Alekseevna will not go with you. If he forces you, and I am not strong enough to do anything about it, then I promise you not to go with him, and to stay here with you."

Now it was my turn to throw myself at her and with bitter tears I promised that I would not leave her. My aunt and uncle embraced me and blessed me for my good intentions. Everyone grew calm except me.

There was one week to go before our departure, and my husband came to see his mother, kissed her on the hand, and said, "I want to ask you one thing which I hope you won't refuse me."

"Insofar as it is possible I will never refuse you," she said.

He started to request to bring Vera Alekseevna with us, her being so fond of us. She responded that this was impossible, and that it was not right to take her away from her mother, who was old and weak. "I think that she herself would not agree to leave her mother."

"If you allow it, then I will get her mother's permission," he said. My mother-in-law said that she would not allow it. He responded, "If you will not consent, then I'll decide to take her on my own. She can find her fortune there and marry a good person."

"I cannot forbid you," said my mother. "But if you say bluntly that you will not go without her, then I must inform you that in that case I shall stay here and will not allow your wife to go with you. She cannot live anywhere without me. This is my decision, and understand that it is firm!"[39]

My husband left in a very angry state, and he and his niece talked about something at some length, and she came out with a tear-stained face. My mother sent for her mother and asked whether she really had consented to send her daughter off with her uncle? She answered that under no circumstances would she let her go. "And why should she go everywhere with her uncle, leaving her mother alone in her old age!" They summoned the niece, and seeing that she had been crying, asked why she was so sad. Her mother told her not to think of her own vain intrigues and to prepare to come home with her immediately. Then she was taken away.

In the evening my husband asked whether I knew his mother's decision. I said, "I do."

"And are you going to remain with her?"

"I do not wish to lie to you. I will not go anywhere without her unless extreme circumstances really force me."

He smirked and said, "I know the real reason why you would happily stay here: you had a fiancé before me whom you wanted and to whom you were not given, and you love him to this very day. Of course, then, staying here would be nice for you."

"I assure you in all sincerity that I have no such fiancé, and whoever told you that was lying. I don't understand how you could believe such a thing and repeat such a lie! Ask your mother about me. She knows me better than anyone else. I know who told you: she passes judgment and speaks according to her own fancies, but I am not afraid of anything. My conscience is clear before God and before you. The only thing I will ever be guilty of is adhering to your mother's rules, and I shall do exactly what she orders, knowing that she does not wish her son and daughter ill." He grew very angry and left the house.

Somehow or other we managed to pack and we went on our way [March–April 1773], and I do not remember how I parted from my friends. My poor nanny had grown so weak with grief that she couldn't even walk. At last we arrived at his sister and brother-in-law's house, and they received us very well. I will never forget their love and affection, especially that of my brother-in-law, who, upon seeing my youth and simple nature, endeavored to treat me warmly, and he told my husband, "Love her and protect her: she will be a good and dutiful wife to you." And little by little my husband really did begin to behave better and more affectionately toward me, and I started to love him. During the four months we spent there I never saw him look askance at me, and my love for him grew stronger by the hour, and he saw that. My dear mother-in-law grew joyful at seeing the bloom of our happy life. I was so happy that I even felt less sadness when I recalled my own family and friends, and only occasionally did I regret that they could not see my contentment. My affectionate brother was an immense comfort to me, and everyone loved him tremendously. Indeed, my husband loved him as much as I could have asked, not to mention dear mother. And he, too, felt great affection toward her as well.

From there we went to Olonets.[40] When we arrived they sent my husband to Medvezhii [Bear] Island on business, and I went there with him. We went by sea, and made a side trip to see the Solovetskii miracle workers.[41] When we arrived at the island, I was the lone woman and without a maid, but my love for my husband overcame all obstacles and tedium. Also, the road there was very rough. In one place we traveled on foot for twelve versts, and the servants dragged the boats along. We walked through the moss called tundra[42] (moss above, water below) in water up to our knees. I shared all these difficulties with him joyfully! But this voyage was made difficult by the large rapids, through which it was impossible to pass by boat. Still, I was extraordinarily comforted seeing how concerned my husband was about me. And, in some places where it was very treacherous to go, he carried me in his arms.

We lived on the island for nine months, and not once was I put out about eating rotten bread, drinking salty water, washing the linens myself, and cooking fish for everyone. I had a mentor in one of the elders[43] among the workers, who stayed with me until he had taught me everything. Once I had learned how to do everything, he too went off to work, about one and a half versts from our settlement. Even alone I felt quite happy, and in good weather I would sit on the seashore with a book or with some work, and wait there to have dinner. When I saw them all coming home I ran out joyfully to meet them, and I embraced my husband, who responded to my affection with his own friendly greeting, which meant the most to me and comforted me more than anything else. In the evenings there were northern lights. I had never seen such majesty: all sorts of landscapes appear in the sky—structures, columns, and trees of all different colors, and the calm sea mirrored it all. And often times when I looked at this I would think, "Oh, if only my friends were here with me: how they would reveal God's majesty to me, and I would feel even greater joy." Sometimes this thought made me cry. One time my husband noticed that my eyes were red, and he asked what I was crying about. I told him my thoughts at once, since in those days I never hid my inner being from him.

Finally the time came for us to leave the island. They brought reindeer to us, and there was no other way to ride than to have each person sit alone in a sleigh and drive the reindeer. I, too, sat by myself, but not knowing how to steer, I frequently toppled over. I quickly learned how to steer, however, and we arrived at Petrozavodsk[44] and found his mother and my brother to be well. Upon our arrival my husband wanted a rest from the traveling, and so the director of factories, who was his friend, came by personally and together they looked over the plans that had been brought from the mines, and the reports about how things were going, and what sorts of machines there were for pumping out the water. They could never keep up because water flowed in from the sea, and work went on only in summer, when the sun never went down but stood always on the horizon, its rays only gone for a quarter of an hour, and that was night.[45] But in autumn and winter we never saw the sun, and the darkness was horrible. Daylight lasted for only a quarter of an hour, and even then it was like a dark twilight. This was a particularly tedious time, especially in the mud hut[46] where practically everything was soaked through. We even slept in the damp, but during that entire time I was as healthy as anyone could wish. I never laid eyes on anyone except for those who had been with us in the summer. A priest who lived sixty versts away came to see us, but when storms were brewing, even he didn't come. In this whole time we saw but one Lapp,[47] and I was as glad to see him as if he were my close friend.

As soon as we arrived there was a quarrel with the supervisor, and my husband was rude and insubordinate with him, at which point they wanted to apprehend and arrest him. But then he grabbed a pistol and said, "Whoever lays a hand on me will be the first one I shoot!" The next day he was out visiting and they apprehended him and held him at the guardhouse. I joined him and stayed there with him for a week. After a while the supervisor reported to Petersburg, and the order came to send my husband to the head administrators and give him back his sword. They gave the sword to my husband and told him to leave for Petersburg within twenty-four hours, and that he had to surrender his command and his accompanying junior officer Deriabin.[48] "But he [Deriabin] is not here with me," said my husband. "He has been sent to Petersburg with the plans." They were certain that he was still with us, however, so we hid him in the closet, under a dress. They came to conduct a search, and they searched wherever they could. My husband didn't stop them but they didn't find him anywhere, and they posted a guard to watch us pack. This was in the summer, and we packed everything on a wagon and a covered cart. The soldiers stood around and watched. The last thing that we had to bring was the bedding in which Deriabin, too, was wrapped and we succeeded in placing him on the wagon and then left. My mother-in-law stayed with my brother at the factory.

We arrived in Petersburg and went straight to stay with Mikhail Matveevich [Kheraskov],[49] who was at that time the vice president of the College of Mines.[50] Nothing further happened to my husband in the wake of the quarrel and his abduction of the junior officer. The directors liked both of them and they saw that both parties were in the wrong. The junior officer was reassigned to Alexander Matveevich[51] [Karamyshev], who had been appointed to the chemistry section of the Mining Corps.

~ IV ~

Thus began a completely new way of life. My benefactors, upon seeing how young I was, accepted me as a daughter and began to provide me with an upbringing. My lessons began, and they advised me to stay busy all the time, and they even set out a schedule of when to get up and when to start working. Getting up so early was burdensome to me at the outset, because my husband had taught me to get up late and drink tea in bed before washing. I had even begun to neglect my prayers to God, because they were deemed unnecessary. I had stopped going to church regularly, and forgotten all those rules that my mother had given me. I had also stopped caring about the poor and unfortunate, and besides there weren't any opportunities to help them. Now that I was living with my honored benefactors all of this was renewed. They taught me to get up early, to pray to God, and in the morning I occupied myself with a good book, not of my own choosing but one which they would give me.

Up to that moment I had never had the misfortune of reading a novel [roman], and I didn't even know the word. One time there was a discussion of some books that had just come out, and they happened to mention a *roman*, and I had already heard the word a few times. Finally I asked Elisaveta Vasil'evna [Kheraskova] about who this 'Roman' was that she kept talking about, and why I had never seen him. At that point I was told that they were not discussing a person, but books of that name, "but it is not a good idea for you to read them so soon." Seeing my childhood innocence and great ignorance of everything, especially the customs of polite society, they started keeping me out of the way. When they were entertaining a large number of guests I was to sit with my benefactor and father, even though this saddened me at first. They never took me visiting or to the theater or out to fairs. At that point my husband had no authority over me, and he was spending entire days over at the Corps of Cadets. Since he was in a new job, there was a lot for him to do.

This sort of education was altogether new to me. They told me not to say everything that I was thinking; not to put much stock in flatterers; to pay no heed to flirtatious men, and not to develop any close relationships with men; not to select my acquaintances according to my own taste; to love most of all those who tell me my shortcomings, and to thank them for it. "Such straightforward people are your friends [said Kheraskov]. While you are here you have no one besides us, and we are your friends. Seeing that you have been raised with good manners—your manners it seems are meek and gentle— I am sure that you will love me and share all your thoughts with me, your intentions, and even the slightest flutters of your heart, your conversations with others, especially with men. Don't be frightened of my strictness. You will find me to be an indulgent father and friend, and if I do anything unpleasant to you, it is only for your own good and future happiness. I shan't say anything about being respectful and warm to people, because you already are."

He asked me how I had been raised and what rules I had been given, how I had spent my time and how the time was organized. I told him everything. He embraced me and said, "Give thanks to your kind and honorable tutoresses, pray for them and never forget their instructions. Strive to say your prayers faithfully every morning, ask God for His mercy, and every evening give thanks for the day you have spent. Begin every activity by asking your Maker for assistance. Your journey in the world is just beginning, and the path you will travel is very treacherous. Without a guide you will stumble, my friend. Now I am your guide, given to you by God. He who does not journey alone in youth, but has a guide, is fortunate. Will you select me to be among your friends, and will you trust me to be your indulgent father?"

I wept and took his hand, which I clasped firmly to my heart, "So long as this [my heart] keeps beating it shall not stop loving you and calling you dear father and instructor of my youth."

At that time I was fourteen, and from that very day I was under his complete authority. I was told that they would demand direct and complete obedience, submissiveness, humility, meekness, and patience from me, that I must not take any independent actions, but simply listen, stay silent, and obey. I promised everything. . . .

When we arrived they were staying at the summer cottage. They had a very large family, but the harmony among them was such as I had never seen—never even heard of. The eldest in the family was the one whom I called father. I enjoyed life at the cottage. They hadn't yet begun their real work with me, but instead they were acquainting me with their relatives and friends. This state of affairs continued for three months, and I became everyone's favorite. My own family could not have been more loving, and I felt nothing but happiness. I sent word to my mother-in-law about where I was and what was happening, and I set it all out in detail. She was immensely pleased, and she wrote the most heartfelt letter to my benefactors, and she gave me over to their protection. "I am now content," she said. "My circumstances, perhaps, will keep me separate from her for some time, but I know that she will be in good hands." At last we arrived in town, where my education commenced in earnest, and it was so extraordinarily tough for me, that all I wanted was for it to end. My benefactor saw this, but he never lost hope, and just kept on correcting me.

Guests would often drop by and that was very jolly, but I was not allowed to be with them. I only saw them at dinner and supper. Occasionally, on someone's name day, or at a dinner-party ball, they would let me in, but only until midnight. Even that was late for me. When I would take my leave of everyone, they would all feel sorry for me and in my sorrow I would leave as quickly as I could. At times like those I was so angry that I just wanted my benefactor to die. For a long time I could not love him, but only continued to do as he wanted out of fear and shame. He often would embarrass me in front of everyone, regaling them with my foolishness. But within about seven or eight months I began to feel love toward him, and day by day my affection and openheartedness returned.

Finally I began to comment that I would like to be out among the guests. He said to me gently, "Why do you want this, my friend? If it were useful for you I would have suggested it myself. The time will come when you shall be granted all the amusements that are not available to you now, and you will take pleasure in them. If you jump into the whirlwind too soon you'll get dizzy. I know what is best for you, and I see farther than you do, so don't try to interfere." I agreed to everything he said, happily and without recrimination, and finally I grew so used to it that I was not at all enticed by what I saw. It went on this way for a long time, and he became completely sure of my love and sincerity. Then he himself took me to the theater for the first time, and everything there surprised and delighted me. When we arrived home everything was so vivid in my mind, and my head was filled with what I had seen and heard. Then they acted out "Honest Criminal," and Dmitrevskii played one of the roles, and this merriment stayed with me for a good long time.[52] But then a long time passed before they took me anywhere. However, I was spending more time with other people and I would sit among them and do my own work. I grew accustomed to society. If I conversed with men I would recount [to my guardians] everything that I had said, and to whom, and they would offer me edifying comments and instructions. So my time passed quite pleasantly.

I had already been living there about two years when the Turkish truce[53] was declared, and several of their relatives returned from the campaign, and they all lived in the same house with us. My benefactors introduced me as a daughter—that was what they called me—and I was happy with all of them. They all loved me sincerely. My husband was no less beloved in all the family. I might even suggest that I was too happy, that there was nothing left for me to want. I only grew sad when someone among my benefactors was unwell, especially my father. At those times, no matter what merriments were planned, I didn't want to go out for any reason, lest he be left alone at home. I found it much more pleasant to be with him when he was ill than with a large crowd. I saw how he took heartfelt pleasure in my devotion to him, how it cheered and comforted him, and he showered me with the most paternal affection and love. Whenever I was ill he felt incomparable distress, I should say the whole family did, even though I never was dangerously ill while living with them. Out of their love for me they imagined that every illness I had was fatal, and to spare them, I often said nothing when I had a headache or stomach ache. But it was no use: either they noticed that my face was pale or they saw the fever and languor in my eyes, and they would start to ask, "Are you really sick, and not telling us?"

My husband often laughed at their distress and said, "You have spoiled her so much for me that I won't be able to deal with her afterwards."

My benefactor always would get angry at him at those moments, and he would say, "You're a fool and you don't know how valuable this angel is!" And he would often ask me, "Does your husband love you?"

I would tell him, "Why wouldn't he love me? I love him a great deal." And I was speaking the truth, since at that point he behaved very well toward me and loved me. He only spent time with those people who came out to see them.

One morning I happened to be sitting in the parlor with my work. One of the nephews came in and approached me, greeted me, and whispered something or other that I don't remember in my ear so as not to speak aloud in front of the servant. I told him not to do this again, that father didn't like whispering. "Yes, but he isn't here now!"

"It doesn't matter to me whether he is here or not, I do not wish to do anything that would displease him!"

He looked at me with surprise.

"Your submissiveness and caution surprise me."

"What's so surprising about that? You should only be surprised if I were to fail to conduct myself this way, as I should, or fail to adhere to the rules which I have received in this home."

Elizaveta Vasil'evna[54] came in and sat down. Her nephew began to say something to her very quietly, and realizing that I might be interfering, I left the room. After a short time I returned and sat down at my work. Elizaveta Vasil'evna came up to me and, without saying a word, began to embrace me and kiss me and call me her inestimable young child. In response to her maternal affection I began to cry and said, "And you are my inestimable mother and benefactress."

Dinnertime arrived and we sat down to eat. I noticed that my benefactor was looking at me with an unpleasant expression. I guessed at once that he actually had somehow seen someone whispering in my ear.

When I finished eating I usually went to see him in his study. When I went in I asked, "Are you well?"

"I am well. What can you tell me about how you spent the morning? Was it happy?"

"As usual, it was very good," I said. He looked at me very intently and asked, "Won't you tell me anything more?"

"No, dear father, there is nothing to say. It seems to me that you are displeased with me. Be kind, then, and tell me what is wrong!"

"Don't you have any idea?" And my tongue felt so heavy that, aware of my guilt, I did not want to acknowledge it and I repeated my previous answer.

"Then there's nothing for me to ask! Go ahead and get to work! There is nothing for me to say to you today!"

I then left and I scolded myself inwardly for not saying anything, and I resolved to speak up that evening. Evening arrived and I went to say goodnight to him and to ask his blessing, as I always did. He said goodnight to me very coolly, and he did not give me his blessing. My obstinacy persisted, and after again not saying anything I left to go to sleep. But I was unable to sleep the entire night because my insincerity troubled me so much!

I arose early in the morning and didn't go see anyone, but went directly to the study and threw myself upon him with tears in my eyes, "My father, I have angered you, and I know how, but I am not guilty," and I recounted everything to him and assured him that I had revealed the entire truth. "I will not leave you! Ask him how it was and whether I have told you everything exactly!"

He embraced me and said, "I believe you, my friend, and I applaud you for your good sense. But why didn't you want to tell me?"

"I don't know myself. Forgive me, I have been punished enough with suffering, which has not permitted me to sleep all night."

"Here, my friend, you have come to experience what harm is done by hiding things from those who are dear to you. I have been no less upset than you, but now it has all come to an end, and I am certain that this is the last time."

I asked him, "Who told you about it?"

"No one. I saw it myself when I was standing by the door. My dear one, know that my eyes and ears are always there with you."

From that time on I never concealed anything that was going on in my heart and saw for myself the affection of my benefactress' nephew, and the more I got to know him, the more I liked him. At last he became a friend to me and my husband, which he later demonstrated on many occasions. Finally it became necessary for him to go visit his mother for several months, and I was very sad to part with him. The day of his departure arrived. Everyone was despondent, and my aunt cried. We began to say our farewells. He came up to me and embraced me, calling me his dear sister, and then he left. This was all so trying for me that tears welled up involuntarily and I did not hide them. When my benefactor noticed this he summoned me to his study and I gladly went with him.

He asked me, "My friend, why are you crying?"

"Over the departure of my friend who loves me so much."

"Why isn't anyone else crying over him?"

"Obviously, they don't know how to love and feel in this way."

"I know that we all love him a great deal, and he deserves it. But there are other nephews here who also love you and can be your friends."

"No, my father, of course they love me, but I am unable to love them as much, and they cannot replace him."

"But he won't be gone all that long."

"I know, that is my sole comfort, and I will be very joyful when the time comes for us to await his return."

"My dear friend, don't you think that this friendship might have unpleasant consequences for you?"

"It gives me nothing but heartfelt pleasure, and I cannot imagine what unpleasantness it might bring."

"But I can. Tell me, did you marry for love and with pleasure?"

"I neither hated him nor cared for him, but only married him to fulfill my mother's wish."

"And if he had been obliged to go somewhere without you, would you have mourned over him and begun to cry?"

"No, and I would not have become melancholy."

"Why not?"

"Because I was not strongly attached to him, and he was not affectionate with me."

"As it happened, then, you had not loved anyone directly, and you do not know what love is."

"Oh, I know that, and very well. I love you, you know that."

"That is a different sort of love, my friend. You love me as a father and friend."

"And how else should one love, and what other kind of love is there?"

"Tell me whether your love for your departed friend is serene. When he is gone what do you feel?"

"I feel bored."

"And when he is with you?"

"It's kind of a pleasant feeling, but to be honest, it troubles me in a mysterious way. I cannot really describe it."

"You said that you love me a great deal, and I believe you, but what do you feel when you sit with me?"

"Being with you is sheer pleasure!"

"Are you serene then?"

"Very!"

"If I'm not home, then what?"

"I sit with my benefactress."

"And you're not sad?"

"No, not if I know that you are well and content!"

"Why then does this love for this friend so disturb you? Love him the way you love me. It seems to me that you are describing two very different kinds of love. Think a while and tell me how it seems to you."

I was silent for a long time and then I said, "It's true. But what does it mean, then? Is it like that conversation I heard recently—I don't know who was talking—about a man and woman who were in love, but the way they said it, it sounded as if they didn't approve of this love. At least that's how it seemed to me."

"I will only say that were you not married I would try to marry you off immediately to your friend, and as you already have a husband and a worthy one at that, then all your love should go to him. But this love you feel toward someone else can break apart the holy union which joins you to him. It would bring such woe and shame to your husband, and eternal shame and a reproachful conscience to you! I beseech you, my dear one, to be wary of allowing anything into your soft and innocent heart that does not belong there. Strive to love your friend with a quiet love that is free of shame. Make sure you are never alone with him."

When I heard this I became so fearful that my face immediately changed color, and I was silent. He asked why I was so sad. "Doesn't it hurt you not to be able to love him this way?"

"No, my father, I assure you that from now on I shall be very careful not to disgrace myself, and not to lose your love. You have opened my eyes and now that I understand all this, it terrifies me to see that without your help I would not have seen this and would have brought misfortune on myself and maybe on my husband. Why didn't you tell me about this before? You saw that I never concealed my devotion to our friend!"

"My friend, I did not think that my observations were just and I was not brave enough to tell you lest I offend your sensitivities. But his departure made clear to me what was going on in your heart. Don't feel shattered, just be strong and good, and avoid anything that might disturb your contentment."

At that time I was seventeen years old, and I very much felt God's mercy in sending me such a benefactor and tutor who knew how to see into the depths of my heart, who knew how to make me see the horror of vice, and who fortified me in goodness. Where would I have been without him? He pro-

tected me as a weak flower from the wind. I was even protected from having any men speak with me and flatter me, the
way men do when they speak to young women and praise
their pretty faces or nice attire. But all I heard was that everyone called me, "our dear one, our meek one," and there was no
one in their whole clan who did not truly love me. They all
protected me and looked out for me.

The time arrived when their nephew returned, but I was
calm. He showed up while I was sick in bed. My husband was
not at home, he was away on business, but not for long and
not far away. My benefactor came to me and told me about
the arrival, and he asked if I wanted to see him [the nephew]. I
said that whatever he deems best is what will be done. "But
there's no danger. I can say with all sincerity that I am calm!"
However, I did not see him until I was better and began to
leave my room; then he came by to see me.

He was very glad that I had recovered, and he said, "I was
very sad to hear that my friend was ill and that I could not see
her." I said, "I am quite certain that since you love my husband
and consider him a friend, you of course would be concerned
about his wife, and for that both he and I are very grateful to
you." From that time on I delicately avoided his company as
much as I possibly could. He took note of this, but his respect
for me never flagged. My mother-in-law also arrived and
when she saw the entire family, she did not know how to express her thanks.

My happy time was coming to an end. My benefactors began to make preparations to go to Moscow. They were not
leaving all that soon, but my heart sank, and where had all my
joy gone? Melancholy tormented me and my heart froze, and I
could not figure out how I would live and what would become of me. As the time of departure approached I began to
decline a great deal. I stopped sleeping and lost my appetite,
the color went out of my face, so that everyone was worried
about me and kept assuring me that their family members
who remained behind would not abandon me, of which I, too,
was certain. But how could they replace [my benefactors]?
There was only a short time left for me to be with them.

My husband rented an apartment, but I didn't want to move before my benefactors had left. On the eve of their departure I did not sleep, and my benefactor gave me a final lesson in how to live. He restricted my circle of acquaintances to those whom I already knew. He told my husband not to strike up new relationships, especially with strangers, and he told me, "My friend, you are so level-headed that you will not do anything without asking and consulting your mother. She is kind, wise, and loves you." He sent everyone out of the room except me.

"My daughter, I am sad to leave you. Be content and listen to me. Only now are you beginning to live with your husband, and I see that you do not know his habits and inclinations, so I will tell you about him. He likes large and boisterous gatherings. Cards are his passion and he has another vice, no better than cards, and without us there may be no one to restrain him. He will soon find companions who suit his inclinations, and you will be unable to separate him from them. But do your very best to keep your distance from them! There will also be more frequent gatherings at your home, I foresee this, but you should go off into your own corner, and occupy yourself with your work or with reading. Urge him in a friendly and gentle manner to abandon his vices. But if you notice that he doesn't like it, stop and beseech God to save him. There is something else I must tell you, too, although it may disturb your gentle and innocent heart: he may take lovers, and his very own companions will tell you about them to your face, in order to get you upset at him. Don't believe them, and even if you know it is true, don't show them.

"Say nothing to your husband about this vice, even though it will be very bitter for you. Let him continue to believe that you do not suspect him. He will not dare to bring it out into the open, and he will keep it secret from you and show you respect. This is the only way to spare the two of you from having an open quarrel. As soon as you give him reason to feel that you know, you will be helping him remove his mask, he will feel unrestrained, and at home he will no longer be ashamed of causing you misery.

"I request, my inestimable daughter, that you be virtuous

and that you conduct yourself so that he cannot reproach you for anything, and so that you can uphold his good name and honor. His behavior will not bring shame on you or besmirch your honor, but rather it will elevate your virtue and make everyone respect you more. If you stumble and enter into vice, however, you will bring dishonor to him and to yourself, and you will be debased before everyone. Do not complain about him to anyone, no one can help you. Defend him always, if someone speaks ill of him in your presence. After that no one will dare to say anything to you. If your life is tedious, do not seek diversions, but turn to work and reading useful books.

"Beware of reading novels. They will not do you any good and they can bring you harm. You may accept books from my brother, who knows what sorts to give you. Honor and love your mother-in-law, and consult with her, but keep silent, if you can, about things you shouldn't say to her, and don't make her reproach her son. Besides, even if you do not tell her, she will see for herself. Do not abandon my family, go to them, they all love you very much. Visit my brother often, as he loves you no less than I. He will stick by you and will give you advice.

"Regarding the money which has been left for you, try to purchase a home. At least then you will have your own little nook. Otherwise I'm afraid the money will go to card playing. Right now he is Potemkin's favorite and he will often visit him,[55] and I am certain that he will also take you along, especially to Tsarskoe Selo, to Peterhof, and all those country houses where Potemkin goes to enjoy himself.[56] He will spend the time as he pleases, and he will leave you by yourself. You will constantly find yourself in the company of young courtiers who will flatter you and pay you a great deal of attention. Potemkin himself will make bold to show you affection, but look out my friend, you will be in for the greatest test of your life. That path is very treacherous for your virtue, and I cannot offer anyone to guide you except God and your own common sense.

"My dear friend, do not lose sight of the precepts you have received. Your entire future life depends upon your behavior. Try to deserve the respect even of highly placed people. Do not be proud, but don't demean yourself either. Do not listen to men when propriety forbids it, and do not give them the slightest reason to be brazen enough to treat you with disregard or disrespect. Don't be dazzled by high standing, wealth, or gifts, but be content with what the Lord has provided and will provide. If you happen to lose your wealth for a time, then you will still have what is most precious, your virtue, and our Savior will not fail to reward you. He will grant you strength and fortitude, but you must not abandon Him and must always ask His help.

"This is the final lesson that your friend and father offers you, and you, of course, will carry it out! My family will send me news of you, and I know it will bring me nothing but the most heartfelt joy."

I bathed his hand with tears, "I shall do as you say and I shall remember your instructions. Pray for me, my father, that God will protect me!" He embraced me and then wept. . . .

And so, my saddest moment arrived. They left and I asked to accompany them on the ride out of town. My husband went too. Once we reached the designated spot I parted with them, but I don't recall how. I was brought back home, and I felt that I was now alone in the whole world, an orphan without guidance. My mother-in-law comforted me and cried with me. "We shall live together, my kind friend, and we shall pray for your benefactor, and we will carry out everything that he prescribed, and it will seem as if he were here with us. God will help us!"

~ V ~

The loss of my kind benefactors left me inconsolable for a long time, and I grew ill. Their family visited me, and this proved to be a great source of comfort. Finally I began to go out, and I visited my benefactor's brother more than anyone else. We lived very close to him, and I took great joy in visiting him.

My husband began to strike up his own acquaintances. Early
on he met Nar[tov],[57] who introduced him to all the vices, and
in a short time they had assembled a rather large group of companions. They played cards, drank, and consorted with loose
women ...With sorrow I saw my benefactor's prediction being
fulfilled, and tears were my only consolation. My mother saw it
all but there was nothing she could do. She employed all her affection to try to ease my sorrow and shared everything with
me. She tried to interest me in books and work. She asked a
teacher she knew to come and teach me to draw, which suited
my inclination. In good weather she went walking with me,
and when I saw her love for me, I tried to conceal my sorrow
from her, knowing that her own suffering was great enough as
it was. They enrolled my brother in the corps.[58]

Finally the card games began even at our house, and they
would play for entire days and nights. You can only imagine
what I heard: noise, shouting, swearing, heavy drinking. There
were even fights! They would lock the gates and doors, and if
anyone showed up, especially an emissary from the administrator, he would be told that [my husband] was ill and was not receiving anyone. While all this went on I would sit with my
mother in a distant room, and simply cry and recall my [previ-
ous] happy and contented life.

After they left, my husband looked horrible. His body was
swollen, his hair stood on end, and he was all covered with
grime from the money. His cuffs were torn away from his
sleeves. In short, it was the most depraved sight that one could
ever see. It broke my heart to see him. He would go right to
sleep, and the quiet would give me some peace too. When he
would awaken from this fog, his mother would come in and
read him the riot act, thinking that this might make him stop.
He always promised her that he would do better ... But what
could she do? He became secretive in her presence, and he
would lie to her incessantly, frequently saying he had to spend
nights at the Corps because Potemkin was setting him various
tasks. The only good that came of this was that they didn't
come to our house as often.

Within two years the money that had been provided on my

behalf had been spent on cards and women. The possessions we had went the same way. We were left without anything and found ourselves in such a state that we had nothing left to pay for the apartment.

Fortunately for us there was a servant, one of my own, who lived with us and who oversaw our entire household. He never left us in need, and, you could say, he fed and took care of us as much as he could. He even attempted to protect my husband. He found out about all the places where my husband would go, and he knew where he was every day. It often happened that someone would come from Potemkin's [office] to pick up my husband. This man rarely revealed that [my husband] was not home, and instead promised that he would be there. Then he would immediately jump on his riding horse, go find him, and bring him home. To the extent that a bondsman[59] could speak to his lord he did so, and he tearfully tried to hold him back from ruining himself and his unfortunate wife and mother. "You could lose your honor and health very quickly. Your very life is in danger! In that case what will happen to them? I am ashamed to say this but I must . . . Don't you know that your mother and wife have nothing left for their own up-keep or that of their house? For some time I have been sup-plying their needs from my own resources, but soon I too will have nothing. At that point I will go to work, but I shall not abandon them. Even if it's nothing but bread, they shall have it!" And after saying this he would weep bitterly.

My husband listened calmly to all he had to say, and then replied, "I will never forget you and I will consider you a friend. Just don't abandon my wife and mother. I cannot promise you that I will give up this company so soon—that is impossible. My superior is a part of this society and he de-mands that I be, too. He can do me great harm!"

"No, dear father, your superior cannot oblige you to do anything harmful, and you should not be afraid of what he could do to you, as long as you are carrying out your responsi-bilities. Indeed, you have another more senior supervisor, why don't you go to him more often?[60] The truth is that you would rather be with the first, who is leading you astray and most of all has separated you from your wife, who is suffering day and night. Still, the Lord is merciful to her, and He has given her a good mother-in-law who eases matters to some extent and who lightens the sorrow in her heart. But there are times when she herself is no better off than your wife!"

He then threw himself at my husband's feet ... "Oh, my kind lord, do not hasten your old mother to her grave and don't deprive my poor young mistress of her last means of support! Do not be angry at your servant, who loves and honors you and who has made so bold as to offer you advice! My father, you are depriving yourself of a contented and happy life ..."

My husband raised him up, and himself wept ... "I know that you are right and I beseech you: prove your love to me and don't leave my mother and wife!"

"Dear father, how can I not leave them? Soon I will not have the wherewithal to help them; I have already told you this. You won today, I know, so give me [your winnings] for the upkeep of your home, wife, and mother!"

He [my husband] handed over a change purse with five hundred [rubles], and the man took four hundred and left him one hundred.

Although he very much did not want to part with such an enormous sum, he simply said, "Haven't you taken rather a lot?"

"No, dear father, just a little. We are all in debt. We must repay our debts and purchase a great many supplies, and this won't be enough. Oh, my poor mistress! Did your mother think when she gave you in marriage that you would depend for your sustenance on a servant, and that your husband would abandon you!"

My husband was in a hurry to leave the courtyard. He came to me to say good-bye. Sobbing, I simply asked, "For how long am I saying good-bye to you?" He left without uttering a word. But I got dressed and went to see my kind neighbor, who asked me, "My friend, what has brought you so low and made you so thin? Are you still mourning over my brother's departure?" I responded only with tears, and he sighed and stopped speaking.

I also went to the home of our president [Mikhail

Fedorovich Soimonov, President of the College of Mines], where they were fond of me and had been inviting me over frequently. I spent whole days with them. He had a niece about my age, a dear girl, gentle and wise, and we became friends. One day I came to their home and I saw her very despondent. I asked her why. She answered that a wealthy suitor had asked for her hand, and her mother was forcing her to tell her uncle that she would accept him. My heart sank, recalling my life and marriage . . . I advised her to be honest with her uncle, but she was too timid to make up her mind to do so, and she did not want to anger her mother. When I found an opportunity to speak with her uncle I related my entire conversation with her. He thanked me a great deal for showing him such trust. He rejected the marriage, and told his sister that he didn't like this suitor, and even though his niece wanted it, as a father he forbade it, and that was the end of the matter. After this they began to love me even more, the entire family, especially the uncle and niece.

One time I was at their home. They had sent for me and I couldn't turn down their invitation. Even my mother-in-law urged me to go, especially when she saw how despondent I was over not having seen my husband in three days, though I knew from my servant that he was alive and well. I arrived looking very sorrowful and bitter. I tried my best to force a smile, but my despondency was fully apparent. The superior asked me, "Where is your husband?"

"I think he is at work," I responded, and an involuntary sigh escaped from me.

He looked at me very intently. "My friend, you are hiding something from your friends, and there is some sort of sorrow in your heart, which you do not wish to discuss. Let us talk later, when we are alone." They had guests the whole day, however, and I was glad that he never had an opportunity to talk with me. I would not have been able to say anything without my mother-in-law's approval.

When we got home I related my entire conversation. She thought a bit and said, "I think that you may tell him, as long as you ask that he not make trouble for your husband or let him know that you said anything. Otherwise something bad might happen!" The next day I became ill with fever and my illness lasted a month. My husband would come home every night, and he appeared to be concerned about me . . . While I was ill his acquaintances also began to visit me, and one of them looked at me and said, "Oh, how sorry I am for you!"

"Why do you feel sorry for me?" I asked. "I seem to be reasonably happy and content, and my husband loves me."

"That's not so, even if you say it is. If he loved you he would not be away from you for days at a time. Can a husband leave a wife who does not deserve it, and can it be that you don't know that he has squandered all his wealth on women and even let his health get dangerously undermined? And you bear all of this with such dignity! Any other wife in your position would pay him back in kind and would not waste energy grieving over such an aimless husband!"

"I am very surprised that you should be so bold as to say such abominable things about my husband to me. I would not stoop even to think about them, let alone to believe you. How can you be so brazen as to offer advice that would shame me? Perhaps you think that I am young and will not see your perfidy and abysmal lies. If so, you are mistaken! And how can you call yourself my husband's friend after this? I now regret that he has been mistaken about you when he considered you honorable and kind!"

"So you don't believe us?"

"I would be ashamed to believe you!"

"I assure you that this is all true, and if we did not respect and love you then we never would have mentioned it."

"I do not think very much of your respect and love if you set about trying to make me quarrel with my husband! I assure you that you will not succeed in doing so. And let me tell you something else: if you truly loved and respected me, you would stay away from me and would not tell me these things about my husband, even if they were true. Once again, I reaffirm that I do not believe and never will believe you. I know that my husband loves me and I love him and I will not demand that he stay with me continuously. I request that you not harbor any useless pity for me. I assure you that I am never bored and I pass the time joyfully and well. I am quite busy and there never seems to be enough time. So kindly spare me your visits. I have no time for you!"

One of the men shrugged his shoulders. "I am surprised that you don't believe all this. I can even tell you the very place where the young women congregate, and there's a bathhouse rented for the whole summer, and everyone makes merry there."[61]

"Then it must be that you too are part of that company! So why aren't you as hard on yourselves as you are on others! Believe me when I say that you cannot sway me from the opinion I hold of my husband. Let me repeat my request to you to leave me, and you can be certain that I shall not be receiving you here any more." I stood up and left the room, and they went off and never came back. Even when they did come by they were turned away.

I recounted the entire conversation to my mother-in-law. She approved my responses and said, "My friend, you must be patient and pray for him. I again ask you, as your friend and mother, to conduct yourself in such a manner that your conscience will not trouble you and that your husband will be unable to reproach you in any way. The time will come when he will regret it all and he will respect you. I am very guilty before you, my dear friend. Not knowing my son, I brought sorrow upon you at a very young age. If it weren't for me you'd have been happy; but don't blame me, I have been properly punished on your behalf. My heart is never at peace and I am forever tormented over you!"

"Do not be upset, kind mother dear," I wept. "I will never blame you. In your love for me you wanted to assure my happiness, but God saw fit to give me a different fate, so I will submit myself to His decisions and I will bear with it. He has not entirely abandoned me since He gave me you. This is no small matter, that I have in you a friend, a mother, and someone to instruct me!"

This is the time when my benefactors' nephew showed up and found out about everything, from whom I do not know.

He asked me but I feigned ignorance. Since he would come by our home every day, he saw that my husband was never home and so grew more certain that the rumors were true. This infuriated him. He had words with [my husband], and finally he said, "I will tell Prince Grigorii Alexandrovich [Potemkin] everything, down to the last detail. You should try to spend more time with him and with your kind superior! Yet you deceive them by pretending that you are always at work! I see your dilemma, in which your life is in such disarray that there seems no way out. What thoughts do you have for your poor wife and mother, whom you have consigned to suffer and endure all of your unseemly behavior? Did it ever occur to you that your wife's patience could come to an end? What will happen then? There will be no cause for it other than you, and you could lose her irretrievably, and all of us who love her would lose her as well. You have ample opportunity to offer her innocent pleasures. She could go everywhere with you, especially during the summer. The prince loves you, and you could go everywhere with him, and so could your wife. Do not get angry at me for bringing all of this up. It's for your own good and peace of mind!"

From that time on things did begin to improve. We began to travel everywhere [together] and wherever we went we always were given rooms. Even the prince came to love me a great deal, and his entire retinue endeavored to oblige me. And I was very happy: youth makes everything jolly.

One time we were in Tsarskoe Selo, and I was walking one morning with my husband in the garden when we met the empress,[62] who stopped and asked, "Prince, are these your guests? Treat them as such and order a table and some fruit for them!" He motioned for me to approach her and she took my hand. She was then told who I was. From that day on I saw her frequently, all of which fed my pride and vanity, especially when I saw that everyone wished to serve me and looked into my eyes to see what I needed. I received the most noble and respectful treatment. All my needs were met then: the prince sent me everything I wanted.

At his home I became acquainted with a tax farmer[63]

whom my husband had recommended to the prince, and who already held the rank of captain and was enrolled in the regiment. As he got to know me better he started visiting us, and once he saw and understood our situation, he advised my husband to buy a house. And we found one. And he provided some money, but that very evening the money was lost at gambling! I found out about it, but there was nothing for me to do. Our benefactor came and asked if we had bought the home. My mother said, "Not only has it not been bought, but the money has already been gambled away. I put my hopes in your friendship, that this will not go on any longer." Without uttering a word he left and purchased the house in my name, and he began decorating it.

None of this cost us a penny. Furniture, cabinetry, and everything that was needed for a home we received from the cabinetmakers, whose children were in the corps. All the furniture was made of mahogany and draped in damask; mirrors, chandeliers, and other appointments were all received from the makers as gifts. And so we moved into our house, where we found even an entire larder and cellar stocked with wines and everything. And our benefactor was there to greet us. He showed us everything and then handed it over to our servant. He even remembered to provide a cow and domestic fowl. Since he knew that I collected songbirds and flowers, we found an ample number of them there as well.

This is how we began life in our new house, and mother and I were quite happy and contented. Even my husband was very happy. After we'd been there a week I was sitting at a window and said to my husband, "There's only one thing missing: a garden. I would love to have one."

"Then there shall be a garden," he said. One morning, less than a month later, my husband woke me, and we sat beneath the window drinking tea. I looked out, suspecting nothing, and when I saw that there was a large garden at the foot of the window, with trees and flowers and landscaped paths, I didn't know what to think. What magic had created such a complete garden in a single night? The people walking by all stopped and looked at it with amazement. I began to thank my husband and was so joyful at this unexpected event that I didn't believe it myself: was I dreaming? My husband was delighted at my bewilderment, and he finally told me that everything had been prepared long ago, and since he knew all the gardeners at Peterhof, the trees, flowers, and workers were brought in from there. There was a master gardener with them whose son was in my husband's command. So the garden cost us nothing.

Once we were ensconced in our new domicile our life was peaceful. I told my husband, "Now my main wish is for you to be home more often and for us to be happy together. Otherwise, however nice it may be, it is no fun alone. If I'm alone all the time I have no one to share my joy. I am not asking you to share my sorrows; I will bear them alone. You know that my brother is not with us now." (He had already been sent off to the regiment, or he had been enrolled and was still staying in the corps.) [My husband] embraced me and said, "You'll see: I will be with you more often. I know how much you have endured, and to make it up to you I will do whatever I can to bring you pleasure. Be merry and content: everyone loves you, and whoever comes to know you will love you too."

"But how can my pleasure be complete? If you aren't here to share them, even amusements bring me no joy. Long ago that scoundrel Nartov took you away from me, and I do not know if I will ever get you back!"

Tears garbled my speech. "I would gladly trade my present joys in exchange for having you back. I do not know whether you love me."

"Oh? What do you think?"

"I think not. If you did love me how could you go for three or four days without seeing me? It seems you care little for my peace of mind. What am I supposed to think? Were it not for your mother and the rules given me by my benefactor, I do not know what would have become of me."

"What would have become of you? You would simply have found yourself a friend of the heart with whom you could pass the time. You have my permission to do so, and if you want I will choose one for you personally. Throw off your stupid prejudices, my dear friend, which are rooted in the stupid lessons of your childhood! There is no sin or shame in making your life merry! You will always be my dear wife, and I am certain that you will love me eternally. But this is a momentary pleasure!"

When I heard this I turned stone cold, and I could not even stop him from finishing these suggestions, and for a long time I could not even speak. Finally I said, "This is the last straw, to hear such abominable and shameful suggestions from the very person who should be helping me follow the rules I have been given! Instead you want me to forfeit all the respect people have for me! If I did this how would I be able to show my face to those who love me? Oh, how shameless you are! You want to take away the last thing I have. Rest assured that I shall not follow your advice, nor shall I abandon my virtue for anything in the world! You are mistaken when you say that if I took myself a [boy] friend I would still be dear to you and you to me. It's true, I would be as dear to you as I am now, I very much believe that, because you have never had any true love for me. But if I decided to pursue your godless suggestions, you should know that I would cease to love you for good!

"I know nothing about the bestial sort of love, and God save me from such knowledge![64] I want to love in a pure and blameless way. That is what's best for me! Or is it that you want to see me become dissolute so that I won't be able to reproach you? Even without that I never complain to you, and I promise never to do so. Even if I wanted to speak there would be no point to it so long as you did nothing to break off relations with your evil boss. I request only one act of kindness of you: that you do not bring this shameful company into my home. I can expect nothing from these people but insolence and brawls. And please warn the originator of all these debaucheries that he had better not have the brazenness to do anything unseemly in my presence.

"Let me further tell you that I will tolerate no more from him, even if he is your supervisor! I know that you have a kind and honest superior, to whom you do not otherwise go except for your formal responsibilities. But his people love me. Don't make me tell him everything. Protect yourself from shame, and do not fret over me. I have a Guardian, to Whom I have turned for guidance since birth, and Who protects me to this day. It pains me to see you without any law and without rules. I've been your wife for nine years and have never seen you so much as cross yourself. You don't go to church, you do not make confession, and you do not take the sacraments. How could I expect any improvement? Unhappy as I am, I cannot hope to regain my lost serenity! Don't be angry with me. You yourself forced me to say such unpleasant things to you!"

He finished eating and left, and that was the end of it. I didn't see him for two days. I was not particularly sad because I passed the time more peacefully and pleasantly without him and with my dear and honored mother, whose love for me knew no bounds.

One day he said that he would not leave the household but rather wanted to spend some time with me. He gave orders to refuse entry to everyone, and he was uncommonly calm and jolly. After dinner we sat in the bedroom, and I was busy with my work while he sat reading. Messengers came from Nar[tov] to summon him and they were told that he was not home. At last Nartov himself arrived, along with Dmitre[vskii],[65] and he [Nartov] went directly to the bedroom and slid aside the door bolts and opened up the bedroom door. I was so furious that I forgot all sense of decorum, and staying right where I was, asked, "I know you are accustomed to gaining easy access to bedrooms, but have you forgotten where you are? How dare you come in here, where no one is allowed but my husband and me! I deeply regret that my husband has such cheeky and impudent companions! I will not tolerate the slightest bit of insolence from anyone in this world, and I will register a complaint with the appropriate authorities. Don't think that they won't stick up for me! You have already done enough, taking my husband away from me and introducing him to all manner of debauchery! But you may not show disrespect to me!"

He was so struck by this that he didn't interrupt. Then, turning to my husband he said, "Why don't you stop her? How can she speak this way to her husband's superior?"

"My husband cannot forbid me from speaking," I replied. "I know very well with whom I am speaking. We have a higher authority to whom I can turn, who is also superior to you! My house is not a tavern, and people better placed than you visit me respectfully and do not dare enter the sitting room if it is closed. I request that you spare me such abominable visits; I am not used to them and never in my life have I witnessed such offenses as I have from you!"

[Nartov] was so angry that he said, "Now I will not release your brother, and I will not certify him to become an officer! You do not know with whom you are speaking, and who is in a position to do you good or harm!"

"You are mistaken if you think that I am frightened by your threats. My brother will be an officer even without you. It is impossible to expect good from you, and you have already suc-ceeded in doing me a great deal of harm. Please don't disturb yourself, nothing is going to frighten me. I know who I am, and I know who you are, and I will no longer speak with you, but let me just say that if you have the effrontery to barge into my bedroom like a bandit again, then rest assured that I will take my complaints over your head, and I am certain that I shall receive full satisfaction. I will not permit anyone to trifle with me!"

My mother-in-law heard the entire conversation. I went over to her and sat down in silence. My husband came over to me and said, "What have you done! Go make up to him and ask forgiveness!"

"You do me dishonor to suggest that I go to such a person to seek forgiveness. He should ask it of me! I intend to seek protection, and I will register a complaint for these affronts with Prince Grigorii Alexandrovich [Potemkin], and I will say that this was done in the presence of my husband, who did not intervene on my behalf. Won't that bring shame on you? Why are you such a coward before such a lowlife and godless person?"

After this they left, and my husband came back home early in the evening. I was surprised, and he behaved very affection-ately toward me. The next day he began to tell me that I had greatly offended Nartov.

"This again! And he? Did he not offend me too? He spoke

with such arrogance, thinking that I would be as cowardly as you. He was quite mistaken!"

"Now he won't certify your brother as an officer, thanks to you!"

"I will not ask him to."

"He can do me a lot of harm in my position!"

"That's rubbish! He can't do anything to you. Knowing our connection with Potemkin, he doesn't have the nerve, coward that he is. So please don't worry about my brother. I'll arrange it without him and without you."

"We must invite him to dinner," said my husband, "and welcome him here more warmly!"

"Go ahead and plan a dinner if you want, but I will not be home [to receive him]. What do you want to do with me? You may invite him in a week, but no earlier. By then I can arrange things with my friends."

The next day I sent for two acquaintances who were close to Prince Grigorii Alexandrovich, and I asked them to do me a favor and ask the prince to send for my brother and grant him officer's rank. I gave as my reason that I didn't want to ask Nartov who, out of pride, would perhaps not be so quick to act. They assured me that it would be done that very week. And so it was. Three days later they sent for him to appear at the chancellery and took him out of the corps without even requesting certification. The prince himself awarded him the rank of lieutenant and assigned him to the infantry armaments regiment.[66] My brother was overjoyed. Upon seeing this, my husband was very glad too, and the next day he went to thank the prince. When he came home I told him that if he wanted to invite his companion, he was now free to do so, and he should also invite those who had made an effort on my brother's behalf. Within a few days everyone came to dinner at our home, and I thanked my friends for their efforts. Nartov was more polite and quiet than I had ever seen him. Within a week my brother went off to Poltava,[67] and I bade him farewell with great sorrow. Since he knew all about my life, he felt even sadder about me.

Shortly after his departure two of my benefactor's nephews

arrived, who loved me like a sister. They spent every day with me, seeing that I always was home alone, and they frequently found me in tears and were very sympathetic to me in my sorry life. One of them was more attached to us, and he always tried to persuade me to be accepting and not bemoan my fate.

"There are others more unfortunate than you. You have a friend in your mother, who shares everything with you and comforts you. You also have other friends who love you no less and who wish you every good fortune. My friend, are you confident that I sincerely love and respect you, as a dear sister, and that I could not love you more? Then accept the advice of your friend and do not receive many men here. Don't bring any censure upon yourself even though all is innocent on your side. For God's sake do not lose your good name!

"Go more often to see our relatives, who love you a great deal. Remember my uncle's lesson: always love virtue. You lately have been visiting the prince frequently, but guard yourself against flattery and don't trust everyone. Always be on your guard. I have heard great praise about you from the prince himself and from all of those around him. It did my heart good when I heard them extol your behavior, caution, and virtuous modesty. Knowing that you and I are friends, the prince himself has expressed to me his curiosity about your life with your husband, and whether or not he loves you. I responded that your life is very good and you are happy. There are many reasons then why you, too, should take care not to reveal your fate. The main one is that many of them, knowing your distress and seeing you in the flower of youth, will endeavor to compromise your virtue. Heed your friend, who loves you and who only wishes good for you. All of our family takes pride in your behavior and modesty, so don't lose [their regard], but rather reinforce their positive impressions of you. Don't change your behavior and you will be respected by everyone.

"Everyone in the family knows about your unhappy life, and they respect you because you don't complain. I assure you that your patience and virtue will in the end overcome everything. It cannot be (otherwise). This may go on for a long or short time, but in the end you will be happy and you will triumph over your husband, who will be unable to reproach you for anything. That is where you should pin your hopes for good fortune and glory! You will bring such joy to all who love you, and most of all to my uncle, who even to this day worries and prays for you, asking the Lord to keep you from stumbling. If you always conduct yourself in this way, even the most abominable man would not dare to treat you with disrespect! Virtue supersedes vice by far!"[68]

How vividly I felt the value of his friendly advice and saw his great love for me. I offered him my heartfelt thanks and promised to follow his advice. Dear friends, pray that God may fortify my heart with virtue! After this conversation I became much more cautious, and when I was in the company of men I didn't know I avoided any hint of intimacy. During that summer I lived for three weeks in Tsarskoe Selo, where my friend also was posted. He was with us every day, and he was glad to see the respectful manner everyone had with me, including the prince himself.

Princess Viazemskaia[69] also frequented that place. She would see me every day, and she even visited me in my quarters. When everyone saw her spending time with me and treating me kindly, they came to show me even greater respect. I took pride in this advantage I had over others. One time she said to my husband, "Are you aware of your good fortune in having such a wife, and do you know what she is worth?" He grew nonplussed and did not know how to answer, but she herself immediately turned the conversation away from this subject, which he found unpleasant. He was very bored in Tsarskoe Selo, and he dearly wished to be in the city, but I asked those around the prince to do me a favor if they could and have the prince keep him here a while longer. I requested this under the pretext that I was very happy there, and enjoying the fresh air, but in actual fact I wanted to keep him away from company that I found so odious and that was harmful to him.

The time finally came for us to go back to the city, and as soon as we arrived he went off to Nartov's and visited the corps. The same life he had led before started up once again . . . He even began to bring people into our house. Very often a game of cards would carry on for about three days. I had made up my mind not to say anything, even though he had already begun to be cross with me. One time I was obliged to spend an entire night in the company of the gamblers, and I witnessed their brawls and heard all the abominable talk of drunken men. But I was not bold enough to leave until one of the gamblers took pity and asked my husband to let me out. Once I left I threw myself on the bed and bathed my pillow in tears. This was my only source of joy!

One day I learned that they had gone off with some young women to Ka[mennyi ostrov][70] to a bathhouse, and that even the president's nephew was there. I went to dinner at his [i.e., the president's] home and resolved to tell [him]. After dinner he went for a drive and invited us to join him. We had just crossed the bridge along the shore when we came across the entire group out for a stroll after their bath, together with the young women. He immediately ordered [the driver] to stop, and he summoned his nephew and my husband and ordered them to sit with us in the carriage. Then we went back. First, he asked who those ladies were with them? They offered no answer, but after we got home, his nephew was placed under guard and was ordered not to leave the house any longer, and my husband was remanded to the corps for two weeks to carry out various tasks. [The president] himself went there every day without warning, sometimes in the morning, sometimes in the evening, so my husband did not dare to be absent. When this ended things got a little better, and he began to be more cautious. Still, he remained angry at me for a long time. He spoke not a word to me for two weeks, but I was patient, seeing that he suspected me of being the reason why the president had gone to the stream near the bathhouse.

St. Peter's name day arrived, and the usual celebration was held at Peterhof.[71] Though I asked many times to go with him he refused to take me and set off alone, early in the morning. I was left all in tears and very miserable. After dinner the elder chamberlain Golynskoi[72] came by, and he expressed surprise that I still wasn't dressed [for the occasion]. I told him that I couldn't go out with my husband. He had left very early to go

to Prince Potemkin's, and he ordered me to find some acquaintances to go with, but all my acquaintances had gone before I had managed to send for them. He offered to let me go
with him. I was very pleased, and I ran to mother and told her.
She looked at me first, and then said, "What are you trying to
do? You know, you will make him furious, and he is already
angry with you!" I began to kiss her on the hand. She said,
"Go, and tell them I sent you!"

I immediately got dressed and left. All the way there I was
happy and contented, but as soon as we got near Peterhof my
heart sank. How can I possibly show my face there? But there
was no turning back now. Finally I said, "I am very frightened,
Pan Golynskoi!"[73]

"But vat are you frightened about? You think they vill suspect me, an old man, of something?"

"No, I am not afraid of that!"

"Vat, then?"

"My husband left me at home and did not want me to go.
So I have deceived you."

"Then vat for did you go? Your husband will have every
right to be even angrier at you for failing to heed him, and
here you have got me, an old man, in some trouble. If I had
learned of this before we had gotten halfway here, I would
have returned and sent you home. Vat is to be done now?"

"You will say that I didn't want to go with you, but that my
mother-in-law was determined that I go!"

"Vonderful! So I'm to begin lying now, in my old age, as a
favor to you, Pani! So be it! Don't be afraid. But you shouldn't
do things that can make your conscience impure or troubled!"

We arrived and went out to the garden. I asked that we hasten to the palace and show ourselves to my husband, so that
no one else could say that he had seen us before my husband
did. And so we went, and found my husband playing cards. He
was astonished when he saw me and said simply, "So, you're
here too? With whom did you deign to come?" I answered
that I had come with Pan Golynskoi. He bowed toward him
very coolly and said, "Why don't you go for a walk? Why suf-
focate in here?" But his face was so angry that my heart froze,

and I was not at all glad that I had come. We went into the garden, and whenever I would come upon one of my acquaintances they would ask, "Are you well? You don't look well at all." And my companion would say, "You are so pale that the only explanation can be that you are very sick. This is what has come of your deception and this unpleasant trip! You have punished yourself, but now we must figure out how to correct the situation."

"Do me a favor," I told him. "When we leave for town ask him to sit in your carriage. Come with us and spend the night at our house, and ask him not to be cross. He likes you and will listen to you!"

At three o'clock we saw him leaving and we went up to meet him. Without looking at me he said, "I am going now. If you wish to stay, you may do so." I said that I did not want to stay and that I would go with him. We left the garden and we sent some servants to find our carriages. Golynskoi asked him to ride in his own carriage in order to travel more pleasantly. My husband looked at him and said, "I know that she put you up to this." With some difficulty he managed to persuade him.

So we sat in his carriage, and while we were there my husband gave vent to his feelings. We both remained silent. Finally Golynskoi said, "All right, you have said enough biting and harsh words to your wife; now permit me, an old man, to say something. Of course she vas wrong to have made the trip without your permission, but I assure you that she had your mother's permission to go, and ven she arrived here she vas very distressed indeed. [This holiday] happens in a year only once. How can you punish a young woman by depriving her of its pleasures! I beseech you, as a friend, to tell me how great is her guilt? Is she always so disobedient before you, or may I intercede on her behalf?"

My husband remained quiet for a long while, and finally he said, "There is no guilt, I simply wanted to test whether she would heed me in this matter, as in everything. This is the first time she has failed to heed me, and for me that makes it all the more [serious]!"

"But do you heed her? Really, shouldn't this be reciprocal? I visit you very often out of friendship, yet I have never seen you obey her in anything. She is obedient and mindful of you in everything. Why do you want to punish her when she isn't guilty of anything? Now I shall put you on the stand: are you right? Of course, she should have borne up before this test, but her youth and vivacious character did not withstand it, and for that I ask you to forgive her. Respect my years!" He then got down on his knees. My husband raised him up, and the old man wept. "If I had not come for her surely she would not have done wrong, and I am sure that she would not have gone with anyone else. But she trusted herself to my advanced years and the friendship which I feel for you!"

At this my husband forgave me and embraced me. I saw that he had stopped being cross and he asked me, "Will you behave like this in the future?"

"No," I answered, "because in the future you will not leave me behind and go to the celebration by yourself."

He laughed and said, "You see, Golynskoi? Not long ago she was crying and fearing my ire, but now what is there to say?" This was said without any anger, however.

"You know that I am sincere and will never give my word if I can't keep it, and you yourself can guard me against anything that is unpleasant for you."

We arrived home, and Golynskoi spent the night with us. Mama came out to meet us, and she scolded Alexander Matveevich for not taking me. "And it was I who told her to go, and you should know that I'll do it again. I'll go with her myself. She sees so much unpleasantness as it is, and yet you still want to deprive her of this innocent pleasure!"

At long last the work assigned by his superior obliged him to be home more frequently. But he was always moping. Whenever I asked if there wasn't some way to make his life more pleasant, and when I would ask whether he would really rather be with other people he would respond, "Do you really think that I can simply exchange you for those young ladies to whom you are referring? You will always be my wife and friend, and the others are just for passing time and pleasure."

"So what is this really all about? I cannot understand how

you can have lovers without love? If this were to happen to me, I would stop loving you. It is a form of bestiality, and it is a sin before God and a violation of the vows you gave to me on the Gospels! Be careful, my friend, that God's justice does not strike you!"

He snickered and said, "How sweet you are when you begin to philosophize! I can assure you that what you call a sin is merely a natural pleasure, and in this I am not accountable to anyone." I began to weep and grew silent, while inwardly I asked God to forgive him.

Several times he tried to persuade me to take a lover of my own and get my stupid prejudices out of my head. I asked him to leave me be with my stupid views and not to speak to me any more about a matter that I found so shameful. "You had the authority to deprive me of my property and peace of mind, but you cannot take away my conscience and good name. God protects me, and He has guarded over me from my mother's womb until this very day. You think as you please, but leave me with my own rules. I assure you, so long as the hand of God protects me, I shall not stray from the path of virtue, and I shall not accept your advice: it would bring harm to my body and soul! Merciful God! The one in whom I thought to find a guide and teacher—he is the very one who wants me to verge from the true path and enter into depravity! But You shall not abandon me, and You shall be my protector! You are my one hope and expectation, and I am certain that as long as I do not stray from You that You will not abandon me!"

I related the entire conversation to mama, who wept bitterly and asked me not to speak with him any more on this subject, and avoid this topic as much as I could.

My entire life proceeded like this, in sorrow, but youthfulness and a joyful nature enabled me to forget frequently about my sorry situation. Every little trifle comforted me. My two friends—one being the nephew of my benefactors, the other being the man who bought us our house—both loved me. Knowing that I love flowers, birds, and all sorts of knickknacks, they comforted me by making a small greenhouse so that in the winter I could enjoy the greenery and flowers. In short, they tried to anticipate my thoughts simply to bring me comfort. Owing to my simple nature I could not think of them as anything other than brothers, so when they came to see me I threw my arms around them with joy, embraced them, kissed them, and called them by the nicest names: friends and comforters. They were affectionate toward me, and frequently, when they noted my innocent demeanor with them, they cried. I was not wary of being affectionate with them in the presence of my mother-in-law and husband—when he actually happened to be home—because my feelings were so pure. At that point I did not know any other kind of love, and I was happy and contented in this. I must admit that I was much more contented when my husband was not home, and even more joyful, and I did not conceal these feelings from my mother.

~ VI ~

So that is how we lived right up until the time when we left for Siberia. He was the one who wanted to go. He asked Prince P[otemkin], as a favor, to make him director of the Irkutsk Bank.[74] It was all he wanted. This was mainly because they had not made him a member of the College of Mines, but had appointed someone else in his place. I asked him numerous times not to go to such a distant spot where I would have no friends or benefactors. If he didn't change his mind, what would I do and to whom would I be able to open my heart and unburden myself? I would have only one friend, my mother, whom I would have to protect, and from whom I would be obliged to conceal much of my sadness. As it was, she had little enough happiness, and her health had begun to deteriorate. "This is the only misfortune that I had avoided up to now, but now you will bring it, too, down on me, and deprive me of my last pleasure and comfort!"

I departed sorrowfully from my home, my friends, and my

benefactors. My brother had already gone off with his regiment to Poltava, and I was deprived of the pleasure of saying farewell to him! My friends tried to persuade [my husband] to abandon this enterprise, but nothing helped. Prince Potemkin himself offered him another position under his command and tried to make him happy, promising to do everything that my husband might require. But [my husband] asked to be allowed to do as he had planned. The prince then reported this to the empress, and it was made official on that very day. An exceptional double salary was appropriated both to him and to all who were assigned to him, according to his request. We sold everything that we had, and did it in a hurry, as if someone were forcing us out. We sold everything for a song.

Early one morning during this time, I went out into the garden with sadness in my heart and looked at my beloved cherry tree, which was covered with flowers, all faded and falling, and all its leaves were turning yellow. I stood there for a long while staring at it. Finally I said, "Dear tree, can it be that you are grieving for me so much that you've lost your beauty and your life is fading? I would want you to flower in my absence, and I hope that your new owner will love you as I do and will take care of you! It is impossible not to love you; you are beautiful and your fruit is sweet!" And out flowed my tears ...

When I went inside I mentioned it to a young man who had been tending the garden out of friendship. He did not believe me and he went out himself, saying, "Just yesterday I watered it myself and was admiring it." When he went into the garden and saw with his own eyes what he had not believed, he was amazed and said sadly, "I do not know if you will be happy and contented where you are going. I fear for you, my kind and honorable A[nna] E[vdokimovna]. I heard from my father, who worked more than forty years as a household gardener, that saplings can sense when they are about to lose a good owner, and if the future holds some sort of unhappiness, they will sense it and die. He assured me that he had noticed this several times in his own life, and now I too fear for you. However, I will look to see whether there are worms at the roots which could be destroying the tree."

He immediately dug it out and examined the entire root. He didn't find anything wrong and the root was reasonably healthy. After this episode we lived there for another month, and the sapling just died; no matter how much he applied his labors and knowledge in hopes of keeping it with him, he just wasn't able to save it.

And so I said good-bye to my friends and benefactors and went off on a distant journey. We stopped off at the village to see my dear and esteemed father and benefactor [i.e., Kheraskov]. We stayed there two weeks while the barge waited for us in the town of Yaroslavl.[75] Saying good-bye was very sad. They grieved and took leave of me as if I had died. I, too, felt great distress when I departed from them, and my spirit fell so low that during the trip to Yaroslavl I hardly spoke a word, and didn't eat, but just lay still the whole time. I was sick when we reached the barge, and stayed in bed for two weeks.

My husband gave me all of his attention and concern and he often looked at me with sympathy and wept, saying, "I seem to have been made to bring you misfortune! You still have seen nothing but misery from me. I have figured out how to take away everything that pleases you, but I cannot give anything in return. Do you believe that I love you, and that you are precious to me?"

I gasped and said, "My friend, up to this point I have seen no evidence of this, but what the future will bring I do not know. I merely ask you to keep in mind that I am now without benefactors, without a brother, without friends. Let me find all of that in you! That would be a blessing for me, and would make me forget everything else in the world and live only for you!"

He wept and said, "My dear friend, it will be so, you'll see, only don't be sad! I will value your peace of mind, and I truly love you!"

"God grant that all this will come to pass, and I would be a joyful creature!"

Finally, I got better. Traveling with us were a chamberlain and paymaster and their wives, who grew very fond of me, and they endeavored to comfort me any way they could. Finally

my sorrow began to pass. My husband became very affectionate toward me, and he did everything he could for me that was
within his power. I grew so optimistic about my good fortune
that I didn't think about anything any more but how to please
my husband, and I tried not to mention anything about our
former problems.

Our entire journey passed in complete contentment, and
eventually we arrived in Irkutsk. They had allocated to us rather
nice quarters. On the third day after our arrival I had a visit
from the governor and the vice governor and his wife, and they
were all remarkably warm toward me.[76] And soon all the ladies
and gentlemen of the area were paying us visits. On the day after his visit, the governor sent a carriage and horses to use until
we got our own. The local merchantry sent over everything we
needed for our home: provisions—vodka and wine, two cows,
and even some hay and various fowl, so I didn't have to buy a
thing. Finally I went out to call on people, and everywhere I
went they received me as if I were some sort of princess.
Everyone liked me a great deal, especially the governor's and
vice governor's families, which pleased my vanity a lot. The
governor really liked my husband, and it seemed that I was
starting a happy life. But my contentment did not last for long.

After we had been there about four months I fell ill, and my
husband had to sleep on the couch. One night, I was lying
there silently, unable to sleep because of my illness, but trying
not to disturb my husband, and I saw him get up very quietly,
come over to me, and ask if I am asleep. I didn't answer, and
believing that I was asleep, he went into another room where a
young woman[77] was sleeping. I then saw all the abominations
he did with her! My heart became very heavy, and I saw how
unfortunate I was. I considered this to be the worst yet, because he had never before had young women at home.

In the morning they brought me tea and my husband was
very solicitous toward me. When he saw that I was very unhappy and that I was forcing myself to hold back the tears, he
began to ask who had upset me and what was going on with
me? I answered that I had a severe headache, but he seemed to
have guessed, and started trying to figure out what I knew. I

was afraid to tell my mother, I didn't know whether she could bear it on account of her weakness, so I resolved to endure and be silent. When the doctor arrived he was surprised to find that I had gotten worse than I had been the day before, and he asked, "What happened to her? She is in a very nervous state, and she needs to be bled this instant!"[78] My husband grew frightened, and mama was extremely upset. So I was bled.

After dinner the governor came to see me, and when he saw me he said, "Could it be that your illness originates in your spirit? Is there not some sorrow in your heart? What I see in your face isn't illness, but grief. I am not bold enough to ask you to be frank with me, because you have not known me for very long, but I would like to prove to you how much I like and respect you, and how much sympathy you will find in me! Come to know me better and you will open up to me. If there is anything you need, just ask!"

"I am not in need of anything except for good advice, and for you to be my tutor and benefactor. Do not refuse me this humble request. Up to now I have never had to live without a friend and guide—but right now I cannot talk to you."

There was a ten-year-old girl living with us who was mama's servant. She helped mama get around and brought her whatever she needed. And he even managed to get at this girl. I wasn't home at the time. He lured her into the bedroom and locked the door, but he was afraid that a shout might bring someone. The girl told her aunt everything, and her aunt told me. What was I to do? How could I help? I was alone; in whom could I confide such horrendous and godless activities? At that very moment my husband came home from the bank, and so the conversation came to an end. Later I thought, "How can I make my husband's shame known, and will any-one here help me bear my misfortune? There is no help other than my Maker! I will ask Him. He will not abandon me!" And I was greatly comforted.

On the third day I got out of bed, and my husband seemed very glad, and he asked our chamberlain and accounts keeper to send their wives around for a visit. They loved me very much, and they never left my side. I will never forget their love. It would have been impossible to keep a secret from them. I had never told them anything, but since we were together every day they figured things out on their own. One time we were at the hay harvest, where we spent a week. There they saw a great deal, how he made advances to the young women and carried out all of his abominations and didn't let anyone get away—neither old women nor young—and they often referred to him by the most unpleasant names. But he felt no shame. He simply forbade them to tell me and threatened to flog them with a whip. Tears were my only consolation. Mama had lost her vision and had grown very weak, and for this reason I could not unburden myself to her.

At that very time the governor sent us to Nerchinsk[79] on the occasion of the death of the director there, to make certain that the silver smelting would continue uninterrupted. My husband wanted to leave me behind, but I didn't want to stay, so I went with him, leaving mama and the whole household under the charge of our beneficent governor.

When we arrived he went off to his work and I began to busy myself with the household. From the very outset I noticed that all the servants in the house had slit nostrils and brands.[80] My heart sank and I grew quite frightened. I was particularly afraid of a certain man named Feklist,[81] who had a beastly face and frightful appearance, and every day he came into the room to stoke the oven. One morning I was still lying in bed when I heard someone come into the room. I got up very quietly and looked through the screen that stood by my bed, and when I saw this horrible Feklist, I fell senseless on the bed and waited for him to come over and kill me, but my lady-in-waiting came in and said that the samovar was ready. I got up and sent for the chief of police and asked him to take this frightful man away. He assured me that he was the very best person among the convicts. "When you get to know him better you will come to love him, but I have no one who is better than him, and I am unable to assign anyone else to his position. Don't worry, I will answer for him!"

After this I calmed down a little, but all the same I could not look at him without fear. I recognized that several of the convicts came from the nobility, and with them I tried to display every possible affection. My mother's sentiments and instructions came back to me, and I vividly remembered all of her good deeds and friendly manner with the convicts, and the way she had included me in them, too. With a joyful heart I undertook to lighten their lot as much as I could, to assist them and endeavor to love them. With these thoughts in mind I went out onto the porch that opened onto the courtyard, where I met Feklist and again became frightened. He stopped me and timidly asked me to listen to him.

I stopped and asked, "What do you need!?"

He fell at my feet. "I see that you are afraid of me. How could you not be? My terrible face bears the marks of my evil doings. But it is killing me that you don't like me. I know that no one can love me, but if only you could come to tolerate me and not be afraid. Christ the Savior has forgiven me. I am bold enough to think, therefore, that I have been given a new heart, and not the beastly one that I had before."

I embraced him and said, "I give you my word that I will endeavor not just to tolerate, but even to love you," and I assigned him to take care of the birds so that he could be with me more often. Shortly after this they came and told me that Feklist was dying, that he had fallen in the courtyard. I went and saw that he was unconscious. I ordered that he be brought into my room, and they sent for a doctor, who bled him. When he regained consciousness, he looked around him, and when he saw that he was lying in my room, he said, "Now I see that you have begun to like me."

I asked what had happened to him. "You still don't know about my evil doings. I was a robber and plied the Volga for seventeen years. What I liked best was to stab people like me and leave them barely alive, and seeing them writhe gave me joy. Today I brought the cook some chickens for the table, and when I went into the courtyard, I looked by chance at the porch near the kitchen and I saw the dead chickens, and they were trembling. My own evil doings came back to me, and all my blood stopped flowing, and I don't remember anything else. So, my benefactress, now you know all about my bad deeds and the reason for my illness!"

So I told him not to do anything that would remind him of his former life, and from that day on he was my favorite, and he deserved it. He was put in charge of the entire household, and whenever we left to go somewhere he would take charge of our rooms as well. He often provided me with opportunities to do good for the convicts, interceding on their behalf and informing me of their needs. I was happy that I was once again carrying out my mother's wishes. I visited the sick, gave as much money as I could to the poor, and visited the convicts in their homes.

They had no prison there, and everyone walked about freely, while some lived in their own homes. One time I went out for a walk with a couple of acquaintances, and we grew very tired. So I dropped in on one of the convicts, a nobleman named Zhilin. When I got to his home I said, "I have come to you so that I might rest and have some tea." He was so touched by my visit that he began to tremble, and he fell down. I couldn't understand what had brought on this reaction. Everyone rushed to help him. Finally, he regained his senses, and we sat him up. I asked how he was feeling, and whether we should send for a doctor, and what had brought on such a bad reaction? "A powerful gladness and sense of gratitude," he responded. "How could I expect such a merciful visitation in my unfortunate circumstances? You are an angel who has brought joy and peace to my heart for the first time in sixteen years! Here is my supervisor's wife visiting me, and that means that he too must not despise me. May the Creator reward you with all good things!"

I was embarrassed to hear such gratitude, and I said, "You say that you are joyful about my visit, but you don't give me tea, and I really need something to drink!" He sat there, all in tears, and we drank some tea. I said good-bye to him and invited him to have dinner with us the next day, and from that day forward he visited me frequently, and went on walks with me. It cheered me that I had provided him some peace of mind, if only for a short time. It takes so little out there to make the convicts happy!

One time when he was visiting me he said, "You have been so good and kind to me that I am taking the liberty of asking you if you could do me an even greater kindness and make a request of your spouse. I have a comrade, also a convict, who lives three hundred versts from here. He and I were exiled for the same affair, and I have not seen him since we began our sentence. Could I not be allowed to see him and spend a little time with him? Let him come to know my generous benefactors and see that even in misfortune a person can find comfort in happiness!" I could not promise, but I did agree to have a word with my husband about whether it could be done. Once when he was in good spirits I took the opportunity to ask him. Under the pretext of going to examine the factories he and I went to the town of Nerchinsk, and he brought Zhilin with him. When we arrived in town, Alexander Matveevich sent for Ozerov,[82] who showed up at once. What a heart-wrenching reunion the two convicts had! So many tears flowed! Both of them fell at my husband's feet and mine, and they called him father and benefactor. And we lived like that a whole week.[83]

Ozerov was well educated. He could play several musical instruments and his behavior was gentle. When we left we brought Ozerov back with us under the pretext of treating an illness: we had a doctor in town who was very good. He then lived with us for seven months, and he left only when it was time for us to go.

When all of them learned of our planned departure, they were so downcast that I could not look at them without the most acute sorrow. They all showed me how sincerely they loved me, if I say so myself. At the time of my departure they were all with me every day for the entire two weeks, especially the convicts. They soaked my hands with their tears, and I cried with them and felt for them sincerely. They were very close to my heart, and there would never be another time like the year and a half that I passed in Nerchinsk. Every day God had presented me with an opportunity to do good for those around me. I fulfilled all of my mother's instructions here: I visited the ill and suffering every day and tended to them. I even had the opportunity to do good for those far away. When the convicts informed me of problems, I even went into the villages to offer assistance.

Oh, how contented my heart was then! My conscience did not reproach me for anything. Even my thoughts were pure, and my husband's shameful transgressions against me affected me less. It made me joyful to know that he could not reproach me for anything. I was not guilty of doing anything against him, and I did not even expose his vices. I was more relaxed in Nerchinsk because there were no women in the house to whom he might turn, and I didn't have to fear that he would lust after anyone. Pretty or ugly—it was all the same to him, so long as there was a woman around.

At last we were ready to go back to Irkutsk, and I will re-member the day we left Nerchinsk until the day I die. All the convicts gathered together at our home, and many of them even spent the night with us. The nobles didn't sleep, and I stayed up with them all night. We spoke very little, and the only sounds were their moans. At five o'clock in the morning the servants brought the horses, and when these servants began arranging things there was a muffled noise and groan. They loaded the horses and we began to say our farewells. At this point [the con-victs] could no longer hold back their sobbing, and all of them fell at our feet and cried, "Forgive us, our benefactors, we are orphaned convicts, and our lot will again become burdensome, and there will be no one to lighten our load! May God reward you and bless you for us, the unfortunate!"

Once we had said farewell to everyone we left. They ran af-ter us with a hue and cry, all in despair. The chief of police wanted to drive them off, but they all cried out, "This time you may beat us, but we will not heed you! Don't you realize what we are losing? Our father and mother!"

We waited, and Alexander Matveevich tried to reason with them, "My friends, you will be as happy and contented as you have been with me. You have a kind supervisor, and he will look out for you. I have put in a good word for you with him, you just have to behave as you have with me!"

"We have behaved this way for a long time, but everything

used to be so bad for us! Before you arrived we were hungry, naked, and barefoot, and many died of exposure. You clothed us, and even lightened our workloads, tended the sick, got us garden plots, made us food each year, and we were no worse off than others. We also know that you have spent a great deal of your own money for us, and that you are departing here not with riches, but with debts. God will not abandon you! This was a loan you gave, and it will be returned to you tenfold by the Heavenly Father! How, then, can you ask us not to mourn? Let us go with you as far as the hills (a distance of eighteen versts)." No one could stop them, and Alexander Matveevich requested this indulgence on their behalf, and we went at a walking pace with all of them, hanging their heads, going on foot.

As we approached the hills they came to a stop, and I cannot describe the amount of sorrow and grief that I witnessed among them. They headed back with a horrible wailing, and an echo repeated their wails . . . I truly do not remember my final moment of parting with them, but my husband wept bitterly. There was a lot of good in him, and it was one of his great virtues that he shared with the poor. Sometimes he would give everything away and keep nothing for himself! This virtue, of course, will bring him credit, and atone for his other deeds.

Our journey took place during a very pleasant time, spring. The places we passed were picturesque: hills filled with fragrant flowers, peach and apple trees. Springs bubbled over from the hills, and they flowed among the flowers through the valleys. They brought back to me similar scenes in Nerchinsk, where I used to enjoy sitting in the hills at sunrise, when the sun would cast its rays on brilliant dewdrops, and all the flowers would raise their heads and give off a sweet fragrance. My heart was joyful in this quietude, and tears frequently welled up even though I did not yet have any real knowledge of nature. I did not find, and did not know how to find and see the Creator in these creations. But even then an inner joy comforted me and eased my emotions. I would return home in such a peaceful state that it seemed that no annoyance could upset me. At these moments all of my mother's lessons and words arose vividly in my memory, and I often spoke as if she could hear me: "My honorable birth mother,[84] here is your daughter carrying out your testament! Of course you hear and see this, and if you can be, you are glad. For a long time your instructions were buried inside me and were not put into practice, and if I depart from here, perhaps that will be so once again. I am here with no guide at all, but may your spirit be my protector!"

Finally, we arrived in Irkutsk. The governor was very glad to see us, and when he looked at me he said, "It seems to me that the air there had a more beneficial effect on you than the air here. You are completely transformed. I see peace of mind in your face. I expected that, since I had news of your life there. I know everything about how you lived and what you did."

"If you know everything," I said, "then who provided me with the peaceful life there, if not you? I credit all of my transformation to you, my honored benefactor. I regret only that I could not live there until the end of my days. Every day brought new joys."

"Don't grieve, you can be happy here too and take pleasure in the delights of life. Think of me as one of your friends and don't refuse me this welcome title!"

"I should be the one making this request of you, and not the other way around!"

"And so, promise me that you will open your heart to your friend, and your secrets will be locked in my heart!"

I burst into tears and said, "Be not just a friend, but also a father. I need your advice and guidance!"

~ VII ~

And so we went back to our old way of life. Mother had stayed in Irkutsk and was very glad to see us. "Was your life there calm, my friend?" I recounted everything to her, and she gave thanks to God that in this short time I had found suste-

nance and pleasure for my heart. "But I foresee that here you
will start suffering again. I ask you as a friend; you are already
in your twenty-second year and I can speak plainly with you.
My dear one, do not let on that you know of your husband's
bad behavior; this is the only thing that can stop him from carrying on out in the open, and your own behavior will make
him afraid to expose what he is doing. I know that you find
this painful and unbearable, but pray to our Intercessor, Jesus
Christ, to send you His aid and patience. He will not leave
you, and He will reward your endurance with great gifts!"

My husband took up right where he left off. The fact that
we were living in very tight quarters—two rooms, and on the
other side two rooms for mama—often interfered with his
lustful pursuits. In light of this, he often sent me away from
the household under the pretext that he didn't want me having guests over who might interfere with his work. I always
obeyed, but if I did not heed him he was extremely cross. At
that point I would flee from the entire scene and leave the
house, mostly to visit the governor. If even that was too much
for me in my sorrow, I went to see our secretary, who lived
outside the city. And there, I could sit by the shore and give
vent to my tears, and she would cry along with me, since she
knew all about my life, not from me but from others. Eventually my spirit grew despondent again and nothing could
cheer me up, even though I made an effort to appear cheery.
Occasionally I forgot myself and my sighs revealed the true
state of my soul.

One time when I was at the governor's, he said to me, "I am
sorry that you live in tight quarters. You really do need a
home. Not far from me there is a house for sale for three hundred rubles. It is very decrepit, but it is a good site and large,
and you could rebuild it."

"Yes, that would be good, but we are in no position to buy it."

The next day the home was purchased in my name, and it
was ordered razed. Logs were brought, and a plan was drawn
up. I was so touched that I couldn't speak, but my tears expressed my gratitude. Our benefactor attended the stone-laying
himself, and he ordered a garden to be planted. They built both

the house and the garden at the same time. He came by every day to oversee the work, and by winter I had a house. Everything that I could need was already there, and our benefactor dined with us at the housewarming.

There were two rooms in the house for me—one a sitting room, and the other a private sanctuary—and they were furnished in the very best taste, not elaborately, but simply and cleanly. He led me into these rooms and said, "Here, my friend, this is just for you. If these rooms can provide you with some small measure of peace in the troubled hours of your life, then I will have already been repaid by you. Here also is Jesus on the Cross, whom you can ask for help and comfort. He will not leave you, just don't you abandon Him!"

Once I was alone my first thought was to go into my rooms and fall before the crucifix and give thanks that He once again had granted me a father and friend in whom I could find my guide and mentor. When my husband saw me in tears he asked, "What has happened to you?"

"My friend, don't take offense. What you see are tears of thanks to my Savior and to our benefactor!"

He too wept and said, "How can we repay him for such kindness?"

"My friend, God does not demand of us anything more than the purity of our hearts and devotion to His will, and that we live in a pure marriage of love and glorify His mercy in our life and actions, and in our pure love for Him. He does not demand words, but looks at our deeds. We shall strive in every way possible to show our benefactor a child's love and gratitude, and we shall be sincere toward him. I must especially praise my Lord: once again I have a father to whom I can open all my feelings, and of course, my heart will be open to him!"

My husband remained seated, and he wept. When he stood up he took a deep breath and said, "Your heart can be open, it is pure, but mine cannot: I must conceal what goes on in it!" He embraced me and went off to bed.

The next morning we both went to see our benefactor to express our gratitude. When I entered his study I wanted to thank him, but I was choking on my tears. He stood up, embraced me, and called me by the most pleasant name, "My daughter and my friend! My Savior sees how much my heart wishes you happiness and contentment. Your peace of mind is closely bound with my own. My heart is open to you, may yours be as well! If I am so fortunate, then you will see in me a friend and father, and you will open your heart to me. As much as I can I will lighten your sorrow and bear it with you, and perhaps my advice will be useful to you!"

He turned to my husband and said, "My friend, you too are dear to me, and I am certain that you love me. From you I demand that you spend every day with me. I do not think that your wife would be displeased by your frequently leaving her alone. I am certain that she will not grow bored, because she has work of her own. And if things do become tedious for her, then she can come and join us. Your subordinates love her very much—this I know—and she will not be all by herself, because they will not leave her. Yes, she is so fortunate that all of them enjoy her company and want to be with her, if that is what she wants."

And so we began to live in our new domicile, but I did not find contentment there. My husband's behavior grew worse by the hour, and I never said anything to him. My mother was already blind, and I tried to conceal matters from her, but she often overheard me crying and asked me, "What is it, my friend, that makes you cry all the time? Even though I do not see, I still hear your tears even in the nighttime. It pains my heart, but I cannot help you. When I had my eyes I could save you from a great deal, but now I can't even get around easily. Pray to the Lord and do not despair. He will not abandon you. Perhaps these cruel experiences are preparing you for something important. Just learn how to endure all of this with humility!"

Very soon after this conversation she suffered a stroke, and she died within a day. With her passing I had lost my last consolation and solace. My husband wept profusely, and I can't even describe what I was like: I was just like a madwoman. My husband mourned deeply for the whole six weeks. After that he began to forget her, and still in the thrall of boredom, he returned to passing time with young ladies, pretending to our

benefactor that he was ill. I often went over to see my kind father, but shame prevented me from telling him about everything that went on. He knew more from the neighbors than I
thought. How often he would have words with [my husband],
who would respond by saying, "I love her a great deal, and she
has no cause to complain about me." Then [my husband]
would reproach me in the crudest way imaginable. No matter
how many times I assured him that I had never said anything
about him to anyone here, he never believed me.

In the end everyone knew about my life, but they could offer me no help other than sympathy. I truly never complained
to anyone, because no one was in a position to help me, and I
kept trying to conceal it all, and to be as cheerful as possible,
knowing that no one likes a mournful face. I was afraid that
they would get bored with me. I poured out my sorrow only
to my father and benefactor, and then only rarely, when I
could no longer keep up a cheerful appearance or suppress my
sighs, and tears would well up in my eyes. Only then would I
let flow from my heart the burden of grief that was weighing
me down. But what could he do for me, what kind of assistance could he offer this suffering woman other than sympathy? Often he wept with me, cajoling me to endure and to
submit to God's will, "My friend, it's not hard to love a kind
husband, but find a way to love and respect such a husband as
yours. Your tolerance will not go unrewarded. Pray to Jesus on
the cross, that He might protect you from all temptations. Do
not entrust the secrets of your heart to any man who can find
a way to exploit them. If someone makes so bold as to speak ill
of your husband to you, forbid it and intercede on his behalf,
and show that you believe nothing that they say about him. In
this way you will bring respect to yourself, and even the most
impudent man will think twice before showing you the least
impropriety."

My husband could not reproach me for anything, as my behavior and innocence protected me. At last he grew much more
affectionate with me, and continued to be so for a rather long
time. Then he became ill. I would sit alone with him in the
evenings. He seemed very sorrowful to me, and I asked him,

"What is troubling you? Is it your illness or something else?"

"I am growing weak. We have no children. My relatives will take back the little village that I own.[85] What will you be left with? This pains me terribly!"

"My friend, you have begun to think about this rather late. There is no help for it now. Don't worry about me, I shall be rich and not poor at all. My conscience is clear before God and He shall not reproach me for anything. I am also innocent before you. Everyone loves me, not because of my merits, but all because of the kindness of the Maker of all that is good. I have this treasure, so what more could I wish for? He has protected me and defended me up to this very minute, so why should He not continue to have mercy on me? As long as I don't abandon Him, He would never abandon anyone who turns to Him, and I have no other helper except Him!"

He looked at me with a grin and asked, "Would you really consider it a sin to have another man besides me who would take my place and from whom you could have children? They would be dear to me because they would be yours, and that would comfort me very much. I could offer you such a person, one I could rely on to keep this secret and protect your honor. And I know that the man of whom I am speaking loves you. Would you really refuse me in this?"

I stayed silent for a long time, because I had turned to stone when I heard what he wanted to bring me to, he who should be my guide and mentor! Finally, I asked whether this was a joke that was upsetting me so much. "No, my friend," he responded. "This is my true wish, and my peace of mind depends on it, and you should not refuse me, but rather you should obey!"

"In everything except this! This is the limit of my honor and obedience to you! I have forgiven everything that you have done against me, but it is impossible to forgive this! What are you trying to turn me into? I know that it hurts you that you cannot reproach me in any way. Rest assured that I learned to be virtuous before meeting you, and none of your threats can make me stoop to dishonorable and abominable acts! You can order me to do everything for you except for this shameful suggestion! I am amazed that you could speak to me about such a matter when you must surely know that I will not heed you!" The flowing tears and sobs choked off my voice . . .

He said, "You are so stupid! I thought that you'd finally gotten smarter. You are now twenty-two years old, and it's about time that you stopped calling something a sin and vice that brings a person pleasure, and I am sure that were you to think about this clearly and find out who this person is, who loves you passionately, then in the end you would gladly agree!"

"There is nothing for me to think about; you have my answer and I have no wish to know the person of whom you speak! It surprises me that you would know about his passionate love for me. If he told you himself, then how could he be so bold as to speak of dishonoring one who is a part of you? But if you brought the subject up on your own, then isn't the dishonor yours? And what sort of person are you making me out to be? Don't think that you can blemish my honor in this way. From now on I will conduct myself more cautiously with any man I meet so that I can be certain in advance that by my behavior I am keeping the most insolent man within the limits of propriety. You have forced me to speak the truth to you, that in you I never had and never hoped to have a guide or mentor. Clearly, the Lord has deemed it useful that people completely unrelated to me would come and instruct me to be virtuous, but from you I have witnessed nothing at all except depravity! You admit this yourself! The Lord has not left me an orphan even here, and He has given me a father and benefactor to whom my whole heart is open, and if you say another word about this to me, then I will resolve to tell him everything about you, and to request instructions from my benefactor about what I can do in such grievous circumstances!"

He became so furious that he began to swear at me and he said, "I have something in store for you that you never expected!"

"I will endure everything as long as the Lord deems it useful to require me to do so. But I will be comforted by the knowledge that I am innocent!"

"You have three days to decide," he said. "Otherwise prepare yourself to see something you've never seen before!"

"Set whatever time limit you wish, big or small; my answer remains the same, and I am ready for everything that you promise me, and nothing will terrorize me. I will know why I am enduring, and patience itself will bring me some measure of pleasure. But I worry about whether you will be content, and whether your conscience will not trouble you for tormenting someone who wants to love only you, though you yourself try to separate me from you!"

Our conversation was interrupted by the arrival of his nephew, who had come to purchase some cloth for his regiment, and he and his wife stayed with us for a long time. All of his relations loved me a great deal and I repaid them in kind, and this nephew in particular strove in every way possible to be helpful to me. From then on I always tried not to be alone, so that this unpleasant matter would not be renewed between my husband and me.

About two weeks passed after the nephew sent his wife ahead to the fortress where his regiment was staying, but he stayed behind with us for a while. One day my husband was not home and I was sitting by myself in my room and thinking very bitter thoughts about my sorry life. I prayed to Jesus, my Lord, to grant me the strength and fortitude to withstand everything that still awaited me. Suddenly the doors swung open and in walked his nephew. When he saw me in tears he said, "Are you going to cry much longer, dear auntie? Be happy. I know about your life and your suffering. So what if he doesn't love you? There are others who know better how to appreciate you, but you don't notice or don't want to notice. All you have to do is say the word, and your wish will be fulfilled!" I could not figure out what he was trying to say, and I asked him to explain more clearly. He began to proclaim his passion directly. I wept bitterly and said, "My Lord and God! Everyone has risen up against me. Protect me! How could I expect such a dishonorable proposal, and from whom? From the one who sees my behavior and knows how dear the purity of my soul is to me! Whatever put the idea in your head and made you so brazen as to say that my husband doesn't love me? Who told you this? If you say that you noticed it from his manner with me, then you are lying. His manner with me is the very best, and in appearance I could not demand more. You cannot see into its inner quality. If your guess were fair, the only thing for you to do would be to pity me, and not to make these abominable propositions, which infuriate me greatly and which in my eyes make you the basest and most contemptible person. You do not deserve for me to speak with you any more. It would be demeaning for me to be with such a person as you! I request that you leave my house forever this very day, and if you don't I will inform my husband and will file a complaint against you with the governor, who is like a father to me, and who treats me as his daughter!"

I was barely able to speak. Sobs stifled me and I tried to leave, but he fell at my feet, begging forgiveness, and said, "I am guilty, but I would never have dared to think of this on my own! Your husband led me to do it, assuring me that you wanted it yourself and that he was in agreement with it. That is why I said that he does not love you!"

My whole being trembled and I could not utter a single word. Finally, I forced myself to gather my strength and said, "Do you think that I believe you? You say this in your own defense and you want to implicate another in this abominable business! There is no point in my staying with you any longer; I have already done you a favor by hearing you out. I hereby request that you go on your way without fail this very day. Now I am going to dinner at my benefactor's and I will not return home until I know that you have gone. If you fail to do this, then I shall reveal everything!"

Having said this I left the room and went that very minute to my father and benefactor. When I arrived, I found my husband there too. When I saw him all of my limbs started to quiver, and I was barely able to stay on my feet. Seeing how pale I was, the governor jumped up, made me sit down, and summoned his wife, who gave me some smelling salts. I said, "Don't worry, I traveled a long way and I'm tired, mostly from the heat. It is over now and I feel better!" I went with the governor's wife into his study, where tears welled up involuntarily and lightened my shame-filled heart. The governor's wife decided that I was having hysterics and she said so to my husband, who guessed what this meant.

After waiting a bit my benefactor entered and with a grieving face asked, "How are you, my friend? I see that something extraordinary must have happened, but I don't want to ask about it now." I merely asked him to keep my husband with him for the whole day.

This is how we passed the time until twelve o'clock. His nephew arrived to say farewell to the governor, and my husband was very surprised that he had decided to leave so soon. The governor explained, "It was long since time for him to leave, and I see no reason for him to stay here any longer!"

After we came home my husband was in a fury, and he spoke not a word to me. I prayed to God and asked for His protection, and then I went to sleep. When I got up in the morning I went to see how my husband was doing. As soon as I went in he asked, "What is the meaning of this, the rapid departure of my nephew, whom I love so much, and who is my perfect friend?"

"You are mistaken in his friendship. He is no friend to you, but more like an enemy, and he is not worth your breath any more!"

He looked at me very angrily and asked, "Why, madam, do you say this, and how can you be so bold as to offend someone when I am certain that he would never do anything that would cause him shame. How has he failed to please you?"

"I have never asked him to please me, it is I who endeavors to be pleasing to your entire family and to do everything that is in my power. It is true, you do have a nephew, K. F. I., whom I not only love, but respect, and who sympathizes with my sorry circumstances and greatly eases my sorrows with his advice. But he would never think of making any proposals that could offend me. Although he is young and unmarried, his rules of honor do not permit him to do something that could wound his conscience. He would not destroy anyone else's peace of mind."

"So who is taking away your peace of mind, and who is making shameful proposals to you?"

As he spoke he looked at me with an intent look in his eyes. I kept silent, but he demanded in a very angry voice that I say why I had come to despise the departed nephew, whom he had wanted to summon here to live. "As long as you force me to speak, you should be aware that I banished him and forbade him from ever coming to my house! He is the one who made shameful proposals to me, and he had the nerve to lie about you, saying you had compelled him to speak and assured him of my impermissible love for him. It was only shame that prevented me from saying anything about this. So after all of this I ask you: is he honest and is he your friend?"

He said, "Why do you think so much of yourself? Even princesses get declarations of love from whoever dares to make them. Even someone who declares an impermissible love gets a hearing!"

"That's a princess only in name, but I consider myself above that and I will not allow anyone to speak to me about anything relating to my honor, much less to yours!"

"Don't worry, madam, about my honor, I know how to defend it myself. But this thing you call honor is merely empty prejudice. There is nothing to prevent you from loving someone else, only do so wisely and discreetly. I have always permitted it and will continue to permit it, knowing for certain that there is no sin in it. It was those stupid women who raised you who gave you these ideas, and your head is filled with every kind of nonsense. I cannot in any way put it out of your head and compel you to live as I would like. Be aware that my nephew will return and renew his quests!"

"Your nephew is not under your command," I answered, "and you cannot give him orders and appoint where he is to live. I will ask my benefactor to move him far away from us, and I will be obliged to explain to him why I am doing this!"

He gazed at me and said, "Is this how you repay my love for you and my friendly indulgence in trying to give you a life of pleasure and comforts?"

"I thank you very much for your love and your permission to do the best things, as you see them, but I cannot permit myself to do this, and nothing on earth can force me to it! You say that the stupid women who raised me taught me this stupidity. So be it! May the Lord help me carry out all their lessons!"

He jumped up in a great frenzy and threw himself at me. I thought that he was going to hit me, but I didn't move from my place. He simply said in the most beastly voice, "Now I know what to do with you! You'll regret it, but it's too late!"

I wept bitterly and said, "I am completely under your power, do whatever you wish. You have authority over my body, but not over my soul! My God guards it against impurity!"

He left, slamming the door behind him, and went to the bank. I went to my room, fell in front of the crucifix, prayed to Him to forgive my husband and not to let me fall, and to give me the strength and fortitude to endure whatever my husband would instigate against me. At that very moment my benefactor walked in, and he found me in a state of severe distress and tears, "My sweet daughter, what has happened to you? What is this sorrow that is weighing you down? Open your heart to your loving father! You yourself have called me by this pleasant name."

I began to sob. "What shall I tell you, my father? I am perishing. Teach me what I may do in this miserable predicament!" And I proceeded to recount everything to him.

He was horrified and he prayed for a long time. Finally he said in tears, "Accept this as a test sent to you by your Lord, be firm and steadfast. With God's help you shall overcome all of this. It will not be a sin to refuse to submit to the will of your husband in this matter, and his nephew will never come here. That much I promise you. This is my friendliest advice for you: pray to the Heavenly Father for aid! He will find the means to save you, and I can only see to it that your husband is in my company more frequently, and perhaps I'll have some success in making something of him. I ask you, my dear one, to be gentle with him as much as possible, and show him how much you love him and are trying to please him. Not just on the surface, but inwardly try to love him.

"It is not hard to love a good man, but you should try to

carry out Christ's law: love even your husband and remember that he too was given to you by the hand of your Maker. His ways are not known to us and it is not for us to put them to the test. Our job is to submit to His rule and not to grumble against Him. If you say that it is not possible to live with him, then think about whether your lot will be better and your soul more at peace if you leave him? Some will fault him, but others will fault you, and more will blame you than him. You are still so young, and will such a change really save you from stumbling?

"It may be that your husband's very cruelty makes you strong and virtuous. Be patient, my friend, and if you do overcome all of this, you will have such joy in the reminiscences of your earlier misfortunes, and you will feel such love and gratitude toward your Savior, Who saved you, fortified you, eased your load, and granted you friends. Is this not a precious gift? He has given you tenderness and patience and everyone's sincere love! There is not a single person who would speak ill of you! But you must not let this go to your head. It is not your own achievement, but has been sent to you by God, so you should turn to Him right this minute with a heart filled with love and gratitude for Him alone. Don't be sad, my inestimable, good girl, don't break the heart of one who loves you as his most favorite daughter! I would be perfectly happy and content if your life were contented. Your happiness is closely tied to my own joy and contentment. My dear friend, be at peace as much as you can, and I will have a word with your husband. He is not a fool, and it seems that he has a good heart, but he has not been guided in the right direction. We shall see what will happen, we shall not lose hope, and you shall pray for him and ask God to show him mercy!"

I tearfully told him, "I will carry out all of your advice and commands, my inestimable father and benefactor! Pray for your unfortunate daughter that her endurance will not weaken!"

He embraced me and wept bitterly and went away, but I was left feeling much relieved. My husband arrived very shortly thereafter, and he learned that the governor had been

at our home. When he came in he asked, "Why was the governor here with you, or did you send for him?"

"I never send for him, but since he is used to seeing us often, he came by to find out if we were well."

"What state were you in when he arrived? Tell me and
don't lie!"

"I have never lied to you and I have no intention of lying.
He found me in tears and in bitter sorrow!"

"Did he ask why you were crying?"

"He asked."

"What was your response to that?"

"That I am unhappy in my life and would sooner have my life
come to an end than live and suffer, and torment my husband, to
whom I would want to bring only joy, and not torment!"

"What did he say then?"

"He ordered me to be patient and to pray for you."

"And are you speaking the truth?"

"I already told you that I will not lie for anything in this
world. Do as your will dictates, believe or don't believe!"

"Beware if you haven't told me the truth. I will find out
from your benefactor himself, in whom you place so much
faith. I will go to him today!"

"Feel free to go and to ask him about everything!"

He looked at me, and after a moment of silence, said, "I repeat that you must make up your mind about my demands, or
else you will have no peace!"

I responded that my mind was made up. I had said—and I
would not go back on my word—that "in this instance I cannot obey you, even if you try to compel me with all kinds of
torture. But you will not force me to do it."

He looked at me and said, "We'll see! I forbid you to visit
your benefactor! Tell him you're sick and do not receive him
or his wife here."

"The first I will obey, but about the second, I don't know if
I can refuse to receive those who are our benefactors. And he
is your superior!"

"It's not your business to give me instructions!" And he left
to dine at the governor's, and he told him that I was ill.

What actually took place there and what the governor told him I do not know, but I really had taken very ill, and my serving woman grew frightened and sent immediately for a doctor, who bled me that minute, and I don't remember anything that happened to me then. The doctor left to go to the governor's and he told them that I was very ill and that my life was in danger. Had he not bled me the consequences would have been dire. My husband became frightened and he ran home to find me in a very weakened state, and with a deathly pallor on my face. Right after him came both of my benefactors, and they sat by me. My father took my hand and found that my pulse was very fast and that I had a high fever. He looked at my husband and said, "So what do you think now? She could even die, and who would be her killer?"

He started to sob and said, "I cannot live without her! She is an angel of gentleness and patience!" He fell on his knees in front of the bed, "Live, so that you might forgive me for all the injustices I have done you!"

I said that I forgave him and would never remember his vexation. "Only your good behavior can erase from my memory forever all the sorrows which you have caused me!"

He said, "I promise you in the presence of your benefactor that I will be your friend and never intentionally offend you!"

Both my benefactors wept and they embraced him and said, "Carry out your promise and be a good husband. Ease her sorrowful life and let her feel the good that you have kept from her!"

Since I was quite weak, they didn't want to talk very long in my presence, and they went with him to another room. Left alone, I thanked my Lord for the illness he had sent me, through which I had reconciled with my husband and saw that he still loved me.

My joy did not last long, however. I lived happily and contentedly for a month, but once again my husband began to live as he had previously, and consorting with young women was his only pleasure. I began to suffer again, but I said nothing to him. My one refuge was in my Maker, that He grant me fortitude and strength. One day he renewed his proposal again that

I choose a lover for myself without fail, "This is what I want."

I answered him, "What happened to the vows and the promises you gave, to make me contented and happy? And why are you speaking to me of something to which I can never be reconciled and which I will never do? I already told you before, and now I will repeat it: I will never permit myself to do anything that my conscience will censure, and I will not bring shame upon those who raised me and instructed me to be virtuous. This is what will make me pleasing to my Creator and dear to other people. I recall all the more the final instruction of my benefactor and father, Mikhail Matveevich!" I then started to weep bitterly, saying, "My father! Do you feel in your heart that your daughter is perishing? You promised to pray for me, may the Lord hear your prayer for your unfortunate orphan!" And I could not say another word . . .

He grew absolutely enraged and said, "I will achieve my goal and tame your cruel and obstinate heart! From now on you will see what will happen to you!"

"I am ready for everything: I cannot expect anything better from you, but my God will protect me from any evil that you will prepare for me!"

He stamped his feet and said, "Be quiet, and don't say another word!"

I stopped talking and my heart was too frozen for me to cry, and I sat like a stone without any feelings. He left the house, and I was barely able to gather my wits: what was I, where was I, and what would happen to me? Tears eased my suffering. I went to mass, and I prayed zealously for my Savior, if it were possible, to take away this evil, with which my husband was threatening me. But if you wish, my God, to permit this evil, then fortify me with Your strength and be my protector!

After this I came home very calm. Before the afternoon meal [my husband] had sent word that he would not be home for dinner, so I ate mine and sat down to my work. Evening arrived and I drank some tea. I did not leave the house because there was a hard frost. And no one came to visit that day, which was very unusual. While awaiting my husband I sat down to read Arndt,[86] but suddenly my heart started beating

hard as if it were frightened by something. Fear so overpow-
ered me that I began to tremble, and my breathing grew labored so that I sipped some water and was sure that something
very bad was going to happen to me. Finally I tearfully began
to pray to my Savior to stay by me and send His help.

At one o'clock my husband came back drunk and extremely angry. He got undressed and lay down. I was already in
bed. At first he began to scold me and call me an undutiful
wife who did not love her husband, and he said that he was
very unhappy with me. I was silent. Finally he said, "Why are
you silent?" He jumped up, pushed me out of bed and had
_____ lie down with him. He ordered me not to leave the
bedroom, but I left anyway. When he saw that I wasn't there,
he got up, swore at me to his heart's content, pushed me out
onto the porch in just a skirt with no stockings, and locked the
door. Partly from grief, but more from the frost, I found it hard
to breathe. Suddenly I saw that someone was coming toward
the porch in response to my moans, and I recognized Feklist,
but was no longer able to speak. He carried me in his arms
and brought me to the bathhouse,[87] which had been heated
up the day before. He wrapped his fur coat over me, stoked the
oven, heated up some water with sage, and gave me some to
drink and wept bitterly. "Our mother, you are the most unfortunate of all! You give us peace while you have none yourself!"

I said, "Pray for me, my friend, that the Lord may take pity
on me!" Then I felt a powerful fever come over me. There
were no tears, but the weight in my chest was unbearable. At
five o'clock the girl came running out, suddenly wondering
where I was. She had been unable to leave earlier. My husband
was awake and he would not let her out of the room, and he
beat her. She rushed over to me, sobbed and cried out, "Is she
alive?" She begged me to put on a warm housecoat, put shoes
on my feet, and then kind Feklist took me in his arms and carried me inside, to the mezzanine, trying not to let my husband
hear us. Here I lay down on a couch and the girl gave me
some tea, which I could barely drink. Other than those two
people, no one knew of my banishment and I forbade them to
tell anyone.

At nine o'clock the next morning I sent for a carriage. When my husband overheard this he came to me and asked, "Where are you going so early?" When he saw my frightful paleness and weakness, he timidly asked, "Oh, mother, what has happened to you?"

I burst into tears and said, "You have no conscience! How can you ask such a question: 'What has happened to me?' You ought to ask whether I am still alive after what you did. And for what? Because I would not submit to you and your abominable wishes. Be advised that I am going to my father and I will tell him everything, and nothing can prevent me from doing this! I have run out of patience, and after this I can no longer live with you. I will spare you from having a wife whom you find odious, and I will demand nothing from you. If I'm left with just the shirt on my back, still my heart will be at peace and my conscience clear. I will not be poor. I have hands and eyes, and God is my helper! I will ask my benefactor to send me to Moscow to my father [Kheraskov], where I will live happily and peacefully. They know me, and they know you too. So do not think that they will hold me to blame. Those who do not know [us] will blame [me], but I don't care about them. You, though, have no cause to reproach me!"

He started to query me and to assure me that he didn't remember anything.

"I only know that this is neither the first nor the last time, and I do not believe that you don't remember. You weren't so drunk that you can say you have no recollection! And there's no point in saying it anyway! I am going, and I will carry through with what I have set out to do, and you can't stop me. You told me yourself yesterday that I made you unhappy and you wished to be rid of me by my death, but I am freeing you even without that, and you will never more have to look upon what has made your life so unhappy. I shall not complain about you, but I will pray to the Lord to forgive you and grant you peace and contentment and happiness in this world and the next! Let His resolution be carried out on me, I shall bear everything with humility!"

It was still early when I arrived at my benefactor's. The pallor of my face revealed to him the state of my soul. I dropped down before him and said sobbing, "Your unfortunate daughter lies at your feet. Teach her what to do and how to arrange her life!" I told him everything that had happened to me. He began to well up with tears himself. He summoned his wife and asked her to give me something hot to drink, because I had developed a high fever. Meanwhile he sent for my husband, who arrived presently. He brought him into the room where I lay and he wept. My benefactor asked him, "Is it true, what I heard from your wife, how tyrannically and basely you have behaved? Has she really deserved this from you? You can tell me directly what she has done to anger you. It would be better for you to break with her if she is not worth your love and respect!"

He sobbed and said, "My benefactor! She is right and I cannot fault her in anything, but help me to beseech her forgiveness! I cannot be happy without her! If she leaves me there will be no one in the world more unhappy than I!" He came up to me and said, "Do you really want to deprive me of life, honor, and peace of mind? Your tenderness and tolerance will not let you do this! Forgive me, I lie at your feet! My benefactor, be my guarantor, join your requests to mine and grant me a new life!"

My benefactor and father came up to me and took me by the hand. His wife, who was sitting beside me, burst into tears, and both of them began to speak, "Your husband is sincerely remorseful, so it seems, and he promises not to cause you pain. My friend, my inestimable daughter, consent to this and heed your father!"

I burst into tears, placed his hand on my gloomy heart and said,

"My father and benefactor, you are the sole consolation of my battered heart! I will do everything for you: I will stay and live with him, even though I do not expect to be happy! I ask only a few favors of him: never to speak to me about a lover again and not to propose anyone; to spare me from seeing what he has compelled me to see. I cannot bear it, and he should let me live in peace. I have never had words with him and never scolded him, but instead I have endeavored to do whatever he wanted, thinking that my gentleness and forbearance would overcome everything. But I have deceived myself completely. Nothing could transform my unfortunate life! Let him say right here whether he has heard me complain or seen my sorrow? Even that I try to keep locked up inside me. My main fault has been that I have put up with everything. Since marrying him I have not had happy and contented days, and those I did have he tried in every way possible to take away from me. And after all of this he says he loves me! I find this kind of love incomprehensible. At least I do not know how to love in this way!

"Tell me now, in the presence of my father, what did I do to you? If I did have words with you, it was not on my own behalf, God knows, but because I was afraid that you would lose your good name. Recall what your esteemed mother said to you through her tears, "Why do you offend your wife and your true friend, and why do you make her so unhappy? You put such a heavy burden and sorrow upon me, too, and this will soon lead me to my grave! Before the Savior I swore an oath to my friend, her mother, that I would make her life peaceful, and I gave her my word that you will be a good husband and friend to her. But is that what I see now? You have been tyrannizing her! While I am still living she will continue to have in me both a mother and gentle friend. But if I die, what will happen to her, poor orphan? To whom will she open her heart and who will share her unhappiness with her? I pray to my Lord to preserve my life, painful as it is to me, but she needs me for her peace of mind. If you do not change your ways you will not find happiness and your conscience will not be at peace even for a minute! I see that you are crying: God grant that these tears be tears of repentance and understanding! I ask you with tears of my own, At least take pity on your old mother, who wishes to live only for you, and don't make my death a bitter one!"

"And remember the day of her stroke, what you were like the day before? Wasn't that the cause of her death? Her old age could no longer bear to see me so unhappy! Even now I cannot bear to think of her loss. With her passing I lost all my happiness irretrievably. She was a mother, friend, and mentor all in one, and the Lord took her from me! His will be done! His ways are inscrutable. She taught me to submit to everything and to endure and still to be grateful to my Savior for these sufferings that He generously sends to me. Can there be any greater torment in life than to have a husband who, instead of friendly contentment, tries to make my life as unhappy as possible? I still have never found solace in you, but the Lord has sent me benefactors who have comforted my sorrowful life as much as they could by their love and friendly sympathy and counsel. I have often envied . . . [*The memoir ends here.*]

The Diary

OCTOBER 1818–JANUARY 1819

[Labzina may have kept a diary for longer than this period, but this is all that has survived. The passages below are heavily excerpted to eliminate much of the repetitiveness of the original, and in order to minimize the number of references to individual Freemasons who otherwise are extraneous to understanding Labzina's writing.]

[OCTOBER] 2.

. . . My whole morning was disrupted yesterday. Because of the holiday, one person after another came by after mass, and I had to take time with them. The last to come was Yuria,[1] and he had dinner with us and was in good spirits, but after dinner he just sort of sat there lost in thought. The children were all busy in their room and came out only after dark. His conversation was all about sister A[leksandra] P[etrovna],[2] how much fun they had at her place the night before. They dined until two, and V[era] A[leksandrovna][3] stayed with them the whole time, and it was very gay. I believe young people must have fun at her place: she has different games, like lotto, "temple of fortune," jackstraws,[4] and they can play with Vera Alexandrovna . . .

My heart suddenly told me that sister A. P. did not love me as I would wish. Sometimes I stay at her place until twelve, and yet she does not give me so much as a piece of bread, nor does she invite us to stay for lunch, though these days young people do get lunch. I blame myself very much for thinking this way; after all, this is a form of envy: "Why don't I get the same treatment as other people?" But if you take a good look at yourself and consider whether you are worth it or deserve even the slightest indulgence, not to mention love, you'll thank God that they even put up with you. And so my heart calmed down.

But here is something else that disturbs it: it is obvious that this divine and holy union has split into two factions,[5] and I find this more than distressing, it is killing my spirit. They themselves make it quite plain who is in which faction: Tuesdays are the appointed day, but who goes? . . . No one, ever. I do not know what will come of all this, or whether God will accept it. He Himself said, "Love one another, and you shall be acknowledged as my disciples." Where is that brotherly love? There is none. What we have instead is cunning and slyness— but against whom? Against [my husband], to whom they should daily confess all their actions. And it was extremely painful for me to hear a young brother even say that "secrecy is sometimes necessary," because someone else's indiscretion could reveal his secret . . . and that was aimed right at A. F. [Labzin] . . . When was there ever such a thing among brothers? I will say, in short, that I live in daily horror and see no end to this misfortune, and my poor husband will be the one who suffers . . .

After this grief and suffering I took up my book of moral lessons, and what did I read, but: "If you lose patience over a minor difficulty, then what will Gehenna[6] do?" It's a weakness of my constitution, o my God, that I cannot bear a painful situation, only in You alone can I expect to find strength, do not forsake me, poor as I am! Lord, I will seek out You alone and open my whole heart to You and fill myself with You. This is all my soul desires, and no creature shall defeat me, and You alone prophesy in me and to me, and I to You. I beg and hope to be united with You and for my heart to turn from all worldly things! Oh when, my God, will I be able to forget myself completely and be fully united with

You and enter into You? Hear, o Lord, the cry of my poor soul and my pining heart, so full of pain!

OCTOBER 3

This morning my head hurts so that I can barely sit up, and my heart is pounding; there are many reasons for this, internal and external. I will never forget the year 1818 as long as I live! I don't think I've ever felt such terrible constraints as I do this year: so much health lost, so much inner life. If only it had befallen me alone, but the O[rder][7] and the brothers—all are in terrible shock.[8] It is no longer a peaceful union, it is now a stormy sea, where many are close to death but don't even think of calling for help, hoping some trick will get them out and unaware that they are wallowing ever deeper toward the abyss. And I—as I watch this, my heart feels endless suffering and grief, the more so as I have no comforter who would want to see my confusion. Even though they keep telling the [brother] who is going so far astray that he should open up to his good benefactor and master, the answer is always, "He will find out, when it is over." They keep telling him, "Then it will be too late: then he will receive the news only as a private person, and he will have every right to be greatly displeased with you." His answer was, "He'll be mad for a while and then he'll stop, I know him!" Thus they use my husband's good heart to evil purpose. He joyfully shares with them all that the Lord sends him in His bounty, but it seems they are already sated and stuffed full, and they go to dainty worldly feasts, where the flesh is satisfied but not the soul, which sits there dozing, and the conscience begins to nod off, too—all the inner world is lulled by the siren's song. And all of this brings me untold horror, and there is no one who will bring it out into the open and reveal the state of that brother's soul since he has immersed himself in sensuality. That is the duty of the first warden, but no matter how much I speak to him he does nothing and makes no move to help. He has a boss, you see. Such a stupid answer, that shows he doesn't know his duty or the importance of his title. They all seem to have become stupid, they know nothing, they hear nothing: for our lawlessness we are deprived of intelligence and light, and all go about with blind-folded eyes, the blind leading the blind—and both will fall into the abyss. Sweetest Jesus! You see through me and know how my poor heart suffers. My only refuge and support and hope, hear my prayer and restore the brotherly union, that they might be sheep of one shepherd. I don't know, my God, what to say or what to ask: my only desire is that all the brothers should go in fear of You and do Your will.

This evening we will be at my sister A. P.'s, where I used to take sweet pleasure in opening my heart, but now she is de-ceiving my husband; though her tongue calls him teacher and parent, yet this is a lie. No one would treat such a person this way, and there are and can be no secrets from him, but she has forced someone else to be secretive and withhold what should be said. I cannot look at her without pain in my heart, because of my love for her. I don't understand who all these tricks and secrets are for. And after all this, how does she value her teacher and with what eyes does she look at him? It is painful and unbearable to see.

So this is my tormented state right now. I have long known that we women were able to make the best and kindest man waver and turn him from his purpose for our own ends, and moreover to make him see it all in the best light and even as Christian virtue: "If the idol of my heart needs this, then I will stoop to it." Given all the cunning and slyness of our sex, a man will never be able to understand a woman, even if he knows her for twenty years. It only takes a month to figure out a man, but us—never. Forgive me, merciful God, for these thoughts, but I have the misfortune to know this from much experience: I've never been led into trouble by a man, whereas women have tried to cast me down into the abyss, and men have saved me.

OCTOBER 4

I spent a very calm and pleasant evening yesterday at my sis-ter A. P.'s. A. F. asked two brothers why they weren't there on

Tuesday. [One] expressed surprise and later asked, "What happened on Tuesday? I didn't hear anything about it." I told him that A. F. receives any brothers who want to come every Tuesday. He said, "No one told me about that," and I am very sorry. It is strange that the brothers don't want to tell each other things, and each thinks only of himself and whether it would be good for him and has nothing to do with the others . . .

I was devastated this morning: the debt-collectors came, and there was no money; that's another thing that is sorely lacking this year. It's just my bad luck; when my sister[-in-law] kept the purse strings, there were nine hundred [rubles] to spend, but I don't even have four hundred. Clearly it's best that I not put my hands to anything; God doesn't give his blessing to anything I involve myself in. I guess my death will put an end to all these difficulties, and everything will get better and there will be an abundance of everything: it is my sins that hold everything back, and the punishment is that nothing works out for my husband and me. What really distresses me is that others are suffering because of me, and who do you think?—those closest to me. Apparently this is God's will that nothing in this world should bring me joy—and not just me: I can't even bring pleasure or assistance to others. That would divert me from worldly things; and there's no other way I'll get away from them. Maybe God's mercy is doing by force what I should do myself, but I just can't improve, even though I see and know all my vileness. This bitterness is a true darkness that envelops someone who does not want to walk in the light. I do not try to realize my Savior's teaching, and I keep resisting with my own life, so how could I be born of God? It strikes terror into my soul to see myself in such a condition. Lord, lead my poor soul out of this dungeon . . .

OCTOBER 6–7

. . . On Saturday I dropped by to see sister A. P. and find out whether the task assigned to her had been begun. It was not only not begun, but the material still hadn't been bought, and now I don't know when it will be. It even pained me that she hadn't volunteered herself. It's already going on two months and now she says there's no money. And when I said we needed twenty-four arshins[9] of satin she became very pensive and, it seems, only wanted to make the large articles of clothing and will scarcely make the things for the small tables. I don't know how it will end, but the sewing should have started by now. Anna Fedorovna[10] [too] would do better not to undertake something at all than to take it on and not do it. That's just it: it's important to think first what to say and what you can do . . .

OCTOBER 8–9

Yesterday I did nothing. In the morning it was guest after guest, and they stayed as much as two hours. My head was spinning and all day I was sort of upset and could not concentrate on anything. There was another guest after dinner, who stayed rather long; when she left I went into the study, but somehow the conversation gave me no peace, it was all about injustices, civil and religious alike. But we can talk all we want, it won't do any good. It is apparent that everything is headed for destruction, though everyone seems to be trying to create and build; they destroy one thing and create another, but nothing is quite right, and they keep trying to make it better, but they seem to start from the wrong end, and nothing sticks. The external is given preference over the internal, and that is why there is such disarray, and anyone who so much as speaks or writes about the internal church is considered crazy or in opposition to the church. It seems that hard and painful times are on their way, and the coming of our Shepherd and Teacher is near.[11] You can feel in your heart the joyful echo of bliss in preparation, and the corporeal world will tremble under great sorrows and persecutions. All you fear is that you might turn away from sweetest Jesus, but again there is the sort of internal faith that He, our Savior, gives us strength, fortitude, and patience and will himself defend His flock, if only we will listen to and follow Him.

The invisible brothers will appear as well—Masons and leaders who will lead and bolster up the weak.

OCTOBER 10

Yesterday evening we rather enjoyed ourselves at a name-day party; the brothers were there, and still somehow something was different from before, as if they do not all serve the same king. There is no true brotherly intimacy; all that remains is an ordinary and polite friendliness.[12] That is what hurts! Where have the former times gone? The old brotherhood is gone. I can say truly that each brother used to be prepared to sacrifice everything for another. What went wrong? The best brother got married;[13] and since then everything has been in flux. That brother's marriage will have an effect: he is also becoming more courteous and close to my husband. Have mercy, my Lord, and spare your poor children! This morning I got up by force of will, my head, but I've started to have severe _____. And my head is better, but I feel a great weakness inside. These days just the slightest anxiety, and this weakness arises inside. It seems we're getting to the point where my aged temple is close to its destruction—all this proves it . . . I woke up this morning with the Biblical text: "Not as I wish, but as it shall please Thee, Thy will be done"—and I got up and crossed myself and said, "Thy will be done, only bless my husband and do not abandon him!"

OCTOBER 15

Yesterday I was very agitated: the drunks were fighting again. This agitation has made my illness worse, and that _____ has started again. Apparently the Lord wants me to have no peace, and to live all day in a sort of fear; my heart was really palpitating, and this morning I had that same _____ again. I don't know what will happen! My spirit does not feel the slightest bit free; it is as if my heart were in a strong and heavy vise; I haven't been breathing freely for a long time; all that fortifies me is the knowledge that I have deserved these sorrows and that my Savior, in His boundless love, wants to purify me.

This is the twenty-fourth anniversary of my happy marriage, but I would like to blacken this year out of my life, that's how easy it was for me. How, then, will the twenty-fifth year begin? May we enter it with the blessing of our Savior and devote ourselves entirely to His holy will. Strengthen us, our Savior, in our true love for You, let us not waver in our hope, faith, and love! Keep our conscience clean, preserve us from false adulation, slyness, and all guile and falsehood. May our hearts be Your temple! You, my God, rewarded me with a husband—a friend and benefactor; in your infinite mercy you rewarded us with friendship and love; may we live thus to the end of our days! May we remain under your direct protection! Make of us Your faithful servants unto the grave! We will love You, Lord, my fortress, Lord our affirmation and our refuge and our deliverer, our God, our aide, and we set our hopes in him, our protector and intercessor! You bless us with your great blessing, thankful as we are to you for twenty-four years of peace and happiness and quiet matrimony, may Your merciful hand stay with us until the grave.

OCTOBER 16

Yesterday did not go the way I would have liked; and I shouldn't have expected it to be as before: the brothers aren't the same as before, and now I see in them a sort of disorderliness and insubordination and willfulness. This is not the same holy union as before, but a republic; and everyone is exhibiting such freedom! Before it was all decent, but now all that is lost: now we have worldly freedom and impudence, which makes the brothers' company unpleasant. What was yesterday like? Like the most disorderly barroom. I used to be able to talk and consult with the brothers in a friendly way, but now they shun me. But sister A. P. thinks nothing of it. At her place anything goes; they got to know her too soon and that is why they act as they do. She never used to see the good side of brother Martynov[14] and always complained of him [to] A. F., but now he's one of her favorites: it is obvious why. This is the sort of faction she is in now: she keeps betraying my husband and turning other people's hearts away, toward their personal interest.

And yesterday was a very sad one for me, it would have been better not to celebrate it at all than to celebrate in such a way. My heart was very constricted and found no relaxation, instead somehow it was closed to joy and pleasure. For this reason my illness revived this morning: this is how weakened my insides are by all these troubles! But it couldn't be otherwise: this internal quivering has been going on not just a week or a month, and I am so flustered I don't know what to do and what to begin! I have forgotten myself completely. Oh, sister A. P.! How much trouble you have caused and how you have augmented these worries: instead of comfort you bring us ever more insubordination and disorderliness! I can't believe that you have not been speaking ill of my husband, your true benefactor. You see everything with different eyes now; your benefactor is not so dear to you now, instead others are closer to your heart. This passion is blinding your eyes, and your judgment will fall most heavily on him who is most injured and who suffers most. O God! Have mercy on us! Bring back the world that used to be in our souls!

OCTOBER 17–18–19

. . . Something else worries me: Katia.[15] Her fiancé[16] is a strange man; he speaks to others but says nothing to us. We were asked to find out from Katia if she was going to marry him. Having found out I told him—and after that nothing. But I know the girl loves him . . . I don't know why they think that I'm not partial to Katia and was saving him for Sonia.[17] God knows that I'm not choosing anyone for my orphan girl, she will have whomever God sends her. But I do know her answer—her heart is open to me—that she has no desire at all to get married, and the married state horrifies her. Yes, it seems there's not much attraction to being a wife nowadays. She will not take that step lightly. After all, it's forever. I have given her fate over to my Lord and to the Mother of God and have no intention to push her or pull her—I think that is an awful thing to do and I'm not the type to do it . . . My Lord takes better care of His orphans than I: He is their father. I'm just glad that she has such a good character. She's smart, careful, and considers all things very clearly and sees purely.

OCTOBER 20

I don't know what this depression is in my heart that I can't get away from! Once more it foretells something and wills me to prepare myself. Thy will be done, my Lord! What disturbs me now is the business with Katia, which is beginning or already begun. I wish it were all clear and out in the open. God grant her happiness! A personality like his will be hard to live with. I confess his character even frightens me. God grant her happiness! But I see that she loves him very much and wants to marry him, and Anna Fedorovna is extremely pleased and apparently sees in him none of what I see. I think she'll have a hard time getting along with his impetuousness. God save her and have mercy! Can her coldness be any help to her . . . I've never seen such a nature: it seems nothing touches her deeply and she takes no one into her heart. What will happen today? He asked to speak with A. F., so they could get his blessing and become a true bride and groom. God Bless this orphan! May she be happier than her mother: her life was so sad, only now can she rest. And all this torments and worries me in the extreme . . .

It also distresses me that the brotherly circle keeps being shaken up: sister A. P. is doing so much mischief. She's like the spark that causes the fire, and no one can put it out. It seems that now every man Jack wants to be a big shot; she's introduced some sort of equality among them, and they are not very obedient to their elders, which never happened before . . . The brothers' dinner at sister A. P.'s was very revealing: this is not a brotherhood, but the wildest republic.[18] And there turn out to be such factions. And the grimaces and whispers! I sat there as if turned to wood.

OCTOBER 21–22–23

I've spent all these days in a sort of awkward situation. The bride is now staying with us, and the groom is with her

every day. I wish Anna Fedorovna were with them more often. I do not like the fact that they always want to be alone,
without chaperones, and they avoid everyone else. Or is it my
depression and inner worries that make me see things going
awry? . . .

OCTOBER 24

My head is so empty that I can neither read, nor think,
nor reason, and I am so weak I can barely walk, but it's
mostly because I can't look forward and see even a shadow
of peace and joy and my heart is very constricted, which
makes my head empty. And nothing good seems to lie ahead
in the whole world. A. F. has no true friend he can talk to,
and his heart is bound in heavy fetters. Oh, how his painful
situation distresses me! But there is nothing to be done: we
must have patience and pray to our Lord for mercy. Our
Savior and merciful God, send our hearts in Thy glory the
spiritual joy to give us strength. [Holy Mother of God]
Refuge of all who grieve, beg Your beloved Son to be merciful toward His weak creatures![19] Your petition and intercession will help us greatly! You have been my hope since my
mother's womb! My parent committed me to your care, my
intercessor and Protectress! Do not abandon us weak ones!
My sweetest Jesus, fortify us with heavenly courage, that this
aged person not be overcome and controlled by the flesh,
which is not yet fully submissive to the soul, and against
which she will still fight as long as the breath of this life remains. What is this life, what is a life that is all full of pains
and miseries, snares and enemies? You pass through one
temptation, another comes; but even while the fight with the
first one is going on, many more crop up unexpectedly. How
can one love a life that is full of so many sorrows, so prone
to miseries and misfortunes? Why is it called life if it brings
only death and sores? However, many do love it and try to
enjoy its pleasures. Sweetest and beloved Jesus Christ! Save
us from the charms of this world, let our only consolation be
eternity!

OCTOBER 25

... Our groom sent word to tell his bride that he wouldn't be coming, and she grew so sad that she put down her work and kept silent and did not speak a word to anyone until he arrived. We sat down to eat. She ate nothing. At last he came at five o'clock, and she grew happy and calm and went out right away into the parlor. God grant that all this will soon be over. They both want to get it over with, do it right now, even. The minutes seem like years to them. I, too, would like to see it end happily, with God's help. He even says, "I won't wait even for the dowry, that is, she can sew it herself afterwards."[20] I don't know, nothing seems to bring me joy. Or, has my heart forgotten what joy is? ...

OCTOBER 26–27–28

I've felt very awkward and could do nothing all these days. My heart was constricted, my head empty, and the soon-to-be wedding makes my head spin, mostly because my husband must come up with the money. They don't care where he gets it; this poor bride has not a thread, and everything must be bought, down to the tiniest detail. It makes my head spin. How much more will a bed cost? It's awful: they don't have a bed, not even a pillow—in short, nothing! I don't know how God will help us and all this is shattering me so that I can't sleep. And what must it be like for my poor husband! It torments my heart to look at him. Fortify him, Lord! The Lord is merciful, perhaps he will send the orphan a pittance from somewhere. But my weakness cannot stand all these sorrows. It's cold today, and it all goes to my heart, which is the source of all my illnesses, and my body and soul grow noticeably weaker day by day, and nowhere do I find anything to build up my strength ...

OCTOBER 29

This morning I got up late and was groggy and sort of depressed. I feel an unpleasant foreboding again! My mind is sort of unsettled today, because once again there is a brother raging against A. F. O God! . . . Bring peace to the brothers' hearts! Light the lamp of love and pure-heartedness in their hearts, and give my husband's heart peace and quiet! He comes to me now and doesn't know to whom to give lodging! This is his payment from the brothers for whom he lives and does not spare himself! All they do is bring him all sorts of insults and vexations; and whomever he favors, that one unfailingly betrays and deceives him. And sister A. P. has repaid him badly for all that he has done for her. Forgive them, merciful God! They know not what they do.

OCTOBER 30

Yesterday was the most painful day for me, and I was unable to take up any work; I went out walking, but the wind was so strong that I stopped at Princess Anna Ivanovna's[21] and she told me many things about sister A. P. She said that A. P. was committing a sin in letting Verochka[22] marry: she is still a child, and she should stay in school. I said I knew nothing about it and it was her will, and A. F. had no part in it and knew nothing. And I was very hurt when she said that A. F. had suffered and lost much because of her. And I myself am the primary reason: I introduced him to her, and he at first wanted to let her go several times, but I kept begging him not to abandon her. I didn't imagine that she still possessed worldly wiles.

It is all my fault now, and my poor husband suffers now because of me. See how wily women are! She managed to deceive me through Jesus the Savior, and I believed she had truly renounced the world and was receiving no visitors, or, if so, they were her husband's friends. And she acted as if she were very tired of it all and always wanted to be alone, and she even exhibited heartfelt pain that she was forced to do all that. But in fact it was not like that: she was still out in the world and her heart was occupied with worldly things. I did see that, but only too late, and I began to warn my husband, but in his kindness and his straightforward heart he did not really believe me, and I could say no more. He even reprimanded me for being of a different mind than he, for not wanting to listen to the clairvoyants, and everyone knew about it at the prince's and elsewhere.

The Lord has brought me heavy crosses to bear in this year '18, and my husband also has not gotten away from it, though the clairvoyants foretold him all good things. Maybe this sin has touched us, too: what is this curiosity of ours, and are we really going to learn something from these peasant women? It all seems like utter nonsense to me, and the Holy Spirit doesn't seem to have anything to do with it. They themselves are deceived, they are blind. What man does, God in his mercy forgives, but He cannot forgive us, for we know more and let ourselves get tangled in lies; we are given to see, through His mercy, something other than what the clairvoyants reveal.[23] They have nothing but flattery, at least nothing I have heard. But I cannot judge them, and even they will not be abandoned by the Lord, because they seek Him and wish to come closer to Him: so how could he abandon them? Each has his own road to follow, but even if we choose different roads, we are all striving toward the same thing and the Lord will lead us all there.

Again I have spent the present month badly: all inner anxieties and bodily ailments, and I did nothing for my soul; especially since Katia was betrothed I have not had a day of peace. Her marriage is somehow terrifying for me, and I have no hope that she can change him; it seems it is not up to her to change him. Will she be happy? I don't know. But I put all that to her and she is still going on with it, and she said, "I can't be happy without him, my heart learned to love him long ago, when I didn't even know if he loved me, and when I saw his tenderness to Soniushka[24] I was afraid he would marry her and I kept crying because I didn't want to marry anyone else." So now it is too late to forewarn her, if she didn't manage to forewarn her own heart. It is already full of love, and she sees nothing in the world but him, and she says her life depends on him. Now we just have to wait for it to be done, for her peace of mind. I pray to the mercy of our Lord, that He not abandon this orphan and that He keep her from all misfortune. She has suffered enough and borne enough, even when she lived with her mother; perhaps the Lord will now give her a better lot.

Now, Lord, I confess to you all my sins of the present month. I did nothing good for myself or for others and was constantly in doubt on all sides and suspicious of Yuliana Egorovna,[25] and she did nothing but lie in every word she said, like some sort of traitor—and many falsehoods came out, but I still do not want to believe it, and God grant that everything I hear about her is untrue. I'm very sorry for her. In all my days I've never been in such a position as I am in now, so how can my thoughts be reasonable! I am constantly worried and doubtful and immersed in my sins. When, o Lord, will you lead me out of this darkness? Do not turn your face away from this sinner, have mercy and bless me as I enter the next month, that my heart may come closer at least a lit. [*No more is written here.*]

THE FIRST OF NOVEMBER, 1818

God bless the beginning month, may I spend it in glorifying You and may my heart and soul find contentment and turn from all the cares of this world; may I bear my Savior's cross with joy and gratitude and love . . .

Yesterday evening my heart quieted down at least a little bit when I heard the reading of "Longing for the Fatherland."[26] And my heart began to long for and crave the approach of the solemn and glorious Coming of our Tsar and Lord. And nothing was dear to me at that happy moment but the glory of my sweetest and most beloved Jesus . . .

And when I went to bed last night I felt both a quiet sorrow and at the same time an unusual sort of peace, such as I had long since forgotten how to feel. I slept peacefully and awoke early and got up in good spirits and with gratitude to my peacemaker, sweetest Jesus. It was just as David said: "He who puts his hopes in the Lord, like Mount Zion, will not be moved." At this moment I am ready for any sufferings, I feel such strength in myself!

Yesterday morning my heart was troubled when A. F. told me that Martynov knew nothing about Fedor Ivanovich's marriage, but I knew that he knew already on April 23. How can a man lie in such company! Kozhukhov and Zhadovskoi[27] knew, they were just afraid that my husband would find out and prevent it. They all are trying to deceive him. And such a pain entered my heart that I came to hate all people and trust no one in the world . . . But, thanks to the Lord, the reading of "Longing for the Fatherland" pushed all hatred from my heart, and now I pity them, like brothers and my true family . . .

NOVEMBER 2

This morning I was disturbed when Alexander said that the coachman had angered A. F. by demanding money for oats—and he had none. My heart went cold: they won't let him turn around before they start bothering, and I know myself what a morning annoyance means—it upsets your whole day . . . I gave orders to take the oats on credit, though they are more expensive here. I don't know how I will manage until my Artemii[28] arrives; he's the one who knows everything, like the right time to buy things, and I am reassured when he is around. The year '18 has been tough for us in every way, both in inner and in external circumstances. What the Lord is trying to accomplish, He alone knows. Thy will be done, my God, only have mercy on my husband, whom You Yourself gave me! Spare this my heart's treasure and do not take him from me; extend his life for the sake of the poor orphans! Oh, how my heart has sunk and aches constantly: I truly never know what to do with myself; nothing can save me from these unbearable sorrows, except death alone . . .

Now they come and tell me there is no flour—and not a bit of money, and all must be taken on credit.

F.K. told me this morning that everything lies embedded in the cross and in death, and there is no other road to life . . .

NOVEMBER 3–4

. . . I was sad that our groom-to-be[29] preferred to dine at A.P.'s rather than at his bride's, even though he knows that A. F. is unhappy with her. But what is more unpleasant is that her spirit is rubbing off on him, he is too impressionable. His char-

acter puzzles me: sometimes he is too affectionate with everyone, sometimes not a word to anyone and no one knows how
to approach him. Yesterday in particular something was clearly
wrong with him. Such gloominess . . . I still don't understand
him, and it makes my heart stop, wondering if Katia will be
happy. His character is not the best, and it is very puzzling. His
wife will have to be very wise to guide and reform it. God
grant that my forebodings deceive me, but she is so much in
love with him that she sees nothing but him now, and I can't
say a word to her about him . . .

NOVEMBER 9

I am terribly disturbed again this morning. Sorokina was
here and all her lies came out in the open: everything she said
was a lie; but for all that I am extremely sorry for her, for she
will now be a most unfortunate woman. My heart suffers for
her terribly, [and] I'm so agitated that my illness has started
again and such agitation inside that I don't know where to go.
This is how easy it is for me! We were sitting at the table and
eating, and brother Bartenev very obviously and incautiously
brought up something that he should not have mentioned. I
was very upset that my dear husband had been so hasty to tell
him about me. He will see that Bartenev will demand that his
wife be inducted too; he has already asked to tell her or show
her the oath . . . He is drowning in selfhood and God forbid
anyone say a word to him—he really dislikes being contra-
dicted. I admit I am extremely afraid to talk to him and I beg
the children to be careful. With his suspicious temper, he
might take anything personally.

NOVEMBER 10

Kozhukhova[30] visited me yesterday morning and I liked her
very much; she seems a very sweet and quiet lady; I've become
afraid to praise anyone—in my old age I keep getting deceived.
Who would think that Yuliana Egorovna and sister A. P. would
have deceived me—and she had railed against her husband and

benefactor; now she herself is suffering and her conscience torments her, so it seems her soul has no rest. I pity her deeply. It's the temptation of her heart's idol; if she didn't have that little girl, none of this would have happened. I don't think she was the crafty one, but her son-in-law to be; now she's under his control and says what she is ordered to say. It will be a bitter trial for her, but she'll hold her tongue and bear it. God grant that I am mistaken! . . .

NOVEMBER 14

Thanks to the Lord, yesterday I felt fairly good in body and in spirit. There was reading in the evening, and I felt quite peaceful. I went to bed and could not sleep for a long time. My thoughts were with eternity, and I was buoyed by the thought that there no one could separate me from my sweetest Jesus. But my flesh began to tremble when I recalled that my husband would be left alone. Who would be able to calm him like this loving heart? This is what keeps me in this world, this and nothing more . . .

My dear Artemii was just here with me and he is amazed that these days there is flattery and cunning even in the rural villages, even among relatives, and the peace and quiet that used to reign there is gone, and God's blessing appears nowhere, and he told us this with such sorrow and he said, "It seems the final days are upon us—there's nothing anywhere but sorrow and constriction; it's painful to see. It crushes me, my mother, to see all this." A peasant man, seeing the end is near—that's delightful.

NOVEMBER 16

I went in great terror yesterday evening to the place where my soul finds its peaceful solace, but praise my Lord, all was fine. It was so sweet that I forgot where I was: I saw the coffin, and death, and our Lady Savior who redeems us from heavy bonds; and everything brought me joy and gave me inner peace. I forgot all the world . . . I do not ask You for honor or glory or wealth or worldly pleasures, I only ask for amity and love and a strong bond between the brothers. This is where my peace, pleasure, and joy lie; this comprises my whole life; I live for love among the brothers; without that love I am dead both in spirit and in body. It seems that great joy does the same thing to me as sorrow: this morning it had that effect several times, but joy drowns it out and I do not feel pain or weakness or distress: everything is easy and bearable. Thank You, my Heavenly Father and Intercessor, for all your kindnesses, which you pour generously on our little circle . . .

NOVEMBER 17–18

Yesterday was a complete pleasure for me: everyone who had practically stopped visiting came to see me, and they all seemed satisfied and happy; only Verochka was very unhappy, and I pity her so much that I couldn't even look at her. What sort of wife and homemaker can she be? . . . It's one extreme or the other: [sister] A. P. used to pamper her so, and now she wants her to do everything and go everywhere alone! I know how hard and bitter it is to get married at a young age, but I had a kind mother-in-law who lightened my load, and even so it was hard and bitter. But yesterday sister A. P., seeing her working with the unmarried girls, said right away, "Vera Alexandrovna, come sit with us, you're a lady now and should get used to sitting with us." She sat down right away—and her eyes were full of tears . . . Why force it on her? It will happen of its own accord; there's no need to take that little pleasure away from her now and make her hardened to her new state. God grant her happiness and peace!

In the evening we sat in the study and read the most consoling thing for the soul. I had the thought that I need a great cleansing for my sins. The Lord's mercy will begin to cleanse me on the other side of the grave, if only my soul will not forget over there His unbounded love and mercy, and will cry out to Him for forgiveness. Beyond the grave the crosses are awful and heavy, but even there He will help us carry them. And with these thoughts I fell asleep, but something woke me and my heart was beating hard, and I couldn't sleep for a long time; I only fell asleep toward morning.

NOVEMBER 19

...Yesterday evening I thought to fortify my strength by listening to the reading, but A. F. went with brother Chiliayev to sister A. P.'s. So I was left alone again. As the saying goes, when everyone has left, then even Tom is a nobleman in solitude; but I wasn't strong enough to go with them, and I waited up until one—they had supper there. May God keep me isolated a long time and let my husband be calm. It's better—much easier—that I endure all this, than to see him worried . . . For some reason I feel very sorry for sister A. P.: she is despondent somehow and is letting her housekeeping fall to pieces. I hope things don't get worse for her later on! Oh, how I pity her! She is so thoughtless about everything. Whatever she had—promissory notes and the rest—was given away even before the wedding. Now if she needs so much as a kopeck, she has to beg it from them. This really was unwise—that's why it was kept secret from A. F., so he wouldn't prevent them from taking everything from her: if only she still had the money that was in the bank for her . . .

NOVEMBER 20-21

These days there have been people here all morning long and I couldn't get anything done. And my thoughts are all mixed up. I am deeply worried about Filakh,[31] I think it's almost a matter of theft with him. But what can you expect from a drunkard? And his wife is dissipated and lazy, she's the cause of all this, and it worries me so much that I can't describe it . . .

NOVEMBER 28-29-30

On my birthday I felt so bad that I didn't even want to be alive. A. F. was very disturbed by Petr Ivanovich,[32] and I truly wasn't sure how I could even walk and thought for sure I wasn't in a condition to go with A. F. I prayed to my Lord only to allow me to be there, where my soul is calmed and my spirit takes comfort. And as soon as we arrived, weak as I was, I started to help brother Martynov and felt such strength that I myself couldn't believe it. And I felt such lightness that it seemed I wasn't sick and the weakness was gone; and as soon as the service began I went into such an ecstasy that I forgot everything in the world and it seemed that all my past and future sorrows were gone. My tears fell like hail, and I greeted them with joy, like precious guests who had long since abandoned me; this relieved me even more inside, and I came home so healthy and calm, it was as if I had never been sick. What freedom inside and in all of me, as if a terrible weight had been lifted from me.

DECEMBER 1–2, 1818

I did not begin this month too well. Something is wrong with me again; that melancholy is back again, and the weakness. How else could it be—they never let me rest. Zakhar[33] made such a racket that I thought it was God knows what crisis. He was drunk and beat his wife and children in the corridor. I sent to inform the police chief and began trembling so much myself and became so hysterical that my arms and legs grew numb and regained feeling only by rubbing them hard. It's as if they are trying to kill me, but I didn't tell A. F. because he already has so much sorrow in his heart from all sides, and I would just be adding to it. Better to bear it myself. But my nerves were so wrought up that the slightest thing could make me tremble. A. F., having paid Korshunov for boots, did not want to pay twenty rubles for my shoes, and I don't have a kopeck, and where will I get it? I was so miserable, my tears fell in rivers; this helped me a bit. Now I need warm boots, but there's nothing to pay with. The girls have no shoes. I had hoped to get something for my birthday, but that hope is gone. Now I don't know what to do, and I don't dare ask. We need so much for the dowry now, who cares about my needs? I was miserable at that minute, but then it passed; I can stay at home when it is cold, and get the girls' made on credit, and so I calmed down . . .

DECEMBER 4–5

I had just started my reflections when guests arrived and I had to leave off; and I was very vexed that there was not a corner where I could find solitude. When you are quiet inside, then things outside don't bother you, but when there is no calm inside, you keep searching for a quiet corner and just can't find it . . . And the harder you try, the worse it gets, and when you see and feel that you don't have the strength to do anything, then the Lord gives his blessing. But I rarely remember to submit to my Savior in everything and to thank Him for everything. I am so sad this morning that I can't do anything. My heart aches so much that it takes my breath away and I seem to be awaiting some misfortune. If I hear someone's quick footsteps, I get frightened; if someone speaks loudly, my heart starts pounding and I can barely catch my breath; and the hardest thing is that I must hide all my sorrows inside, so as not to grieve my loved ones. Let me suffer alone and endure it all: why should they?

. . . Yesterday A. F. and I visited Mrs. Vasilieva, and I don't know, nothing interested me and I was very bored. From there we went to see Andreevskaia, whom we found very ill. And I do not praise her for exposing her husband's great dishonesty. What will she accomplish by that, and how will she live with a dishonest husband after that? By revealing his dishonesty she loses her own reputation. I would rather die than tell anyone in the world about my husband's wrongs. Whatever he might be, he's still my husband! Or else I should leave him altogether after that. She's doing a bad thing, and I truly don't know how to judge them; it's the sort of secret I can't understand. Mightn't she have given him cause for all this? Oh, how difficult it is to judge a husband and wife, and God knows which of them is right. I avoid all this as much as possible. What sort of judge am I of others' affairs? Though she's talking about it, she insists no one tell him and keeps him from knowing what she told me, and even insists that

I alone know this secret and have no right to make it known; I have my own sorrows and I am torn up inside by many anxieties, so God save me from interfering in others' business. God be with them. I know very little of what's in the letters, either; she showed them more to Alexa., and there's nothing in them but complaints that they have abandoned her . . .

DECEMBER 8–9

What sorrow and misery are in my heart, it is beyond my ability to express it! My spirits are so low again that my body is suffering as well. I truly do not know where to turn; I can't read or write or work or anything; again prayers don't come— that is the worst torment, that I am not vouchsafed to give prayers to the Heavenly Father.

Something is starting up again with sister A. P. God grant that it be to the benefit of my loved ones; but I am so accustomed and trained to expect deception that all ventures terrify me more than they give me hope. My heart will tremble with terror for my husband: may his name not be dragged further down than it is already! What else can you expect from these female acquaintances. God grant that I be mistaken, but my heart foresees something very unpleasant. Lord, give your servants patience, but somehow we have brought these crosses upon ourselves and must bear them. God grant that we not bring even greater ones upon ourselves—but that does seem possible: we irrationally poke our noses in everywhere where they don't belong, without thinking twice, and we often rejoice at things that lead us to our destruction, and afterwards we regret it and grieve. Oh, man, man! Examine yourself well, and you will find that no one is the cause of your spiritual ills but you yourself— you are your first and most dangerous enemy, wary of others but not of yourself, and if you were to examine yourself and beware of yourself as a strong and dangerous enemy, then you wouldn't drive peace from your heart. I cannot manage my own heart: it hasn't completely reconciled with sister A. P.'s slyness. If she had been crafty and deceptive with me, I truly would not have interfered on my own behalf, but all this is done against my husband, who does not see it and does not want to see it—so I pray to the Lord to keep it hidden from me, too, to make me just as blind in this case, so that these storms might not arise in my poor heart and I might be calm . . .

DECEMBER 10–11–12–13–14–15–16–18

I have been very unwell all these days in soul and body, and have been unable to get started on anything. My grief has been such that I haven't known where to turn, and my spirit is so constricted that I can barely catch my breath! How long, my God, will your anger continue, and how long will you turn your face from this sinner? There is no Sun, and no warmth. I'm like ice all over, nothing interests me, nothing delights me, I have lost the favor and the paradise of my Sweetest One! I don't know how I can get it back. I can't sleep at night, and if I do fall asleep, then I sleep very heavily and my grief is with me the whole time. There's not a single thing that can bring me any joy at all. It used to be that my Lord's mercy brought me joy inside, which overcame all external anxieties, but now I do not have that blessing. Clearly I have deprived myself of it, but I don't know how. I've let external things make me very anxious and have ignored the inner things, and it has all come out on the surface. This is why I have lost my whole inner world. It is easy to lose it, but getting it back is hard.

On Sunday I was very upset again because A. F. went visiting Outside . . . ; my heart trembles to think that rumors may start up again in town, and may go even farther; just now it was calming down. They will recount it to their own honor that A. F. was visiting them, especially that talebearer. What am I to do, since this upsets me in the extreme; it would be better if they said it of me, rather than of him, and it seems to me that these rumors will be a hindrance to him. Or has my poor heart grown accustomed to fearing everything? I have become so nervous and timorous when it comes to my husband that I make an elephant out of a fly. I don't think it used to be like this for me, but now I'm afraid of everything, and besides, they didn't used to say such things and there was nothing for them to say. It is impossible for me to be healthy or calm, and I am sure I will die with this worry and inner anxiety. Right now I feel a strong desire to leave Petersburg and go anywhere else; I am even starting to hate it, though I used to like it. Last year various inner circumstances began to tear me up inside, and my husband became the object of various slanders. I don't know if I'll be strong enough to bear this much longer, or how long my Lord will wish to test me. Thy will be done, my God! You do not send us tests that are beyond our strength. I pray you: put a guard on my lips, that my mouth and tongue not open. It profits nothing to speak: everyone looks at everything with his own eyes and finds his own occupations for his heart, and others—no need to think about it; and how can I give anyone advice? Since I can't figure myself out and I see and feel my own foolishness and my most shortsighted little mind, then it's my duty to keep silent. Last night my husband said to me, "Thank you for instructing me and teaching me, but I know what I am doing." I reproached myself inside for being unable to hold my tongue: in my present condition I should not open my mouth, but should only pour out my heart to my Lord and bring all my sorrows and burdens only to Him . . .

JANUARY 1819

I don't know how I spent the rest of December. I was so grief-stricken by my husband's illness that I couldn't get started on anything until the New Year, and I truly don't know what happened to me. And when he started going out I became sort of shy, especially on Sundays, so that all my blood is stopping within me. And so all this month is gone and I have done nothing . . .

Appendix 1

THE VARIANT BEGINNING TO LABZINA'S MEMOIR

1810—The Description of the Life of One Noble Woman

I was born to honest and honorable parents. My birth brought my parents great joy. Although they had had other children prior to me, none had survived. I was the first one to bring pleasure to their lives, and they prayed incessantly to God that he leave me as consolation to them! I was very precious to them. My parents celebrated my birthday not with balls and dinners but by giving gifts to the downtrodden and aid to all the needy, and they prepared dinners for the downtrodden for three days. My father served them himself: he went around to the prisons and distributed to them what they needed, and he took in two orphans who were held there for upbringing. This is how my honored father marked my birthday. After me they had two sons, but my father loved me the most, saying that I was his first gift from the Lord and "her birth gave me a new life, new feeling. The other children were gifts my Lord gave me for my old age, but my daughter is dearer to me, and I beg the Heavenly Father to be merciful with her, to grant her his blessing and endow her with virtues and to grant her an obedient and humble heart, full of love for those close to her, and even more for the poor."

I did not have long to enjoy the happiness and love of my father. I had just turned five when death took away this beneficent father and friend of the poor. One brother was two years old and the other was ten months old when they became fatherless. With his passing my mother lost all her happiness and contentment. She was left without him, a widow at thirty-one. But my father was seventy-three when he died, after being ill for just eight days. Prior to this illness he had never been sick and didn't touch medications. My mother also had a strong and healthy constitution and she felt ill only while pregnant and giving birth. They had the most joyful life, and God blessed them in everything. Everyone loved them, they had true friends and kind relations, and the visible blessing of God reigned in their home. There was never anyone like a thief or a drunk, and there were no dissolute women, and all the servants loved their master as children love their father, and they were faithful. The death of such a good and beneficent friend, father, and husband left their friends unspeakably sad, and his family in despair. When he felt that death was near he summoned my nanny whom he loved dearly, and who esteemed him as well. "Listen, my friend. I am near the end and I feel that I am dying. I cannot speak with my wife about this, seeing the mournful state she is in, but I ask you as a friend. After my passing tell my wife and friend that my children should be raised to know God, and they should learn from earliest childhood to love Him with all their heart. They should love and honor their mother and obey her, they should have respect and regard for their elders, not only those of equal standing but also good servants. Do not let them fall into bad company, but show them good and Christian examples. Most of all teach them to love the poor and unfortunate and enjoin them to share everything equally. For the sake of God do not teach them about luxury and a delicate diet, but accustom them to a Spartan diet, severe weather, and simple attire. I especially ask you this, my friend, with regard to your young mistress, who is so precious to me and who has been in your charge since the day she was born. Promise me this in my last minutes . . ."

Appendix 2

FREEMASONS' CEREMONY

[The following document is an excerpt from an article[1] by early-twentieth-century scholar Tira Sokolovskaia. In it Sokolovskaia describes a passage from the protocols of the Dying Sphinx Masonic lodge from 1819, discovered in the archives. It relates the lodge's decision to invent a ritual ("the bearing of Masonic gloves") to honor Labzina on the occasion of her twenty-fifth wedding anniversary to A. F. Labzin, the Grand Master of that lodge. Sokolovskaia explains, "By bearing gloves, which in Masonic ritual symbolized frailty and purity, the brothers of the Dying Sphinx lodge, lacking the right to select a woman into their milieu as a lodge member, wished to show their respect for A. E. Labzina and her high moral character."]

A CEREMONY TO HONOR LABZINA AND TO MAKE HER AN HONORARY MEMBER OF THE DYING SPHINX LODGE (1819)

The protocol begins as follows:

"In the year of the true world of 1819, the eighth month, fourteenth day, in the east of St. Petersburg, at seven o'clock in the evening the lodge of instruction[2] was opened by the usual regimen in which the following occurred."

On the fourth point we read:

"Upon the request of the Venerable Grand Master as to whether one of the brothers has a recommendation, the Venerable Deputy Master asked to be allowed to have a word. The Venerable Grand Master handed him the mallet. The Deputy Master accepted it, and he read some words of edification, explaining that the most important responsibility of the brother Freemasons was to have a sincere love for all human beings . . . 'We come to this honorable [lodge] [there follows a sign of the square symbolizing a Masonic lodge],' he said, 'to conquer our passion; to subordinate our will to the laws of the mind, enlightened by the greatest light, which unfurls the Word of God before us; . . . to improve not just ourselves, but others, to be an example to those outside of our society leading them to virtuous acts, and we are obliged to observe all the rules of honesty, truth, and good conduct, by the oath to which we have freely sworn to undertake all the responsibilities imposed upon us by the spiritual and civil authorities, and to carry them out in all their exactitude, and not by appearances alone. All of this very honesty, truth, and good conduct centered in our consciousness is brought to fruition by our own generosity . . .

"'Who has sanctified this temple? Who has gathered us into one? Who is the founder of this and the one responsible for the Fraternal union? Who, by his guidance, leads us in the above duties in a courageous and unflagging manner? The Venerable Grand Master, our Aleksandr Fedorovich Labzin, who up until now has joyously led this our honored [square]. Precisely he and no other. And consequentially we are obliged to him alone for his great love, guardianship, and instructions for us, that all of us are obligated by an indescribable heartfelt gratitude, honor, and humility.'

"After touching on the virtues of matrimony, the Deputy Master turned to the Grand Master's twenty-five years of lawful marriage, which attest that just as the Lord himself had brought a wife to Adam in Eve, so too, he said, 'the hand of God had foreordained holy matrimony for the V[enerable] Grand Master and given him as a wife our truly most highly esteemed sister Anna Evdokimovna, and tomorrow will mark their twenty-fifth year together.' 'Truly,' repeated the Venerable Deputy Master, 'she is our most highly esteemed sister, for by carrying out our seven duties to the letter, she is precluded only by her gender from being our brother. Outside our society she always maintains strict modesty, faithfully carries out her duty to her spouse, is in all things utterly virtuous, harbors love for all humanity as well as for those closest to her, courageously and constantly, with faith and hope in Him Who is near all those who call upon Him. She overcomes all onslaughts of this Evil World with patience, and conquers the most heartfelt injuries with God's aid. She is magnanimous with good advice, gives generously to those in need, whether they ask for it or not, striving as much as possible to anticipate [their needs] with her help, and she cares for many under her own roof, as a faithful assistant to her husband. She considers death to be her redeemer from the burdensome bonds of the flesh, tormented in the vale of tears, and her benefactor who will lead her to the most blessed and eternal life. In short, she has devoted her heart entirely to God, and submitted herself to His holy will and guidance. By following such a path she has become [her husband's] soul mate, therefore she is a fitting model not only outside our society but for us brothers as well. By her example she inspires true virtue.

"'And so,' said the Venerable Deputy Master, 'as we have among us a Venerable Grand Master who excels in knowledge, in talents, and in virtue, and finding in his wife the excellent qualities of strict, exquisite, and holy virtue, we consider today to be a worthy occasion, on the completion of twenty-five years of their union, to bring a spiritual offering of gratitude and prayer to our Creator and their Uniter. Saint Gregory Nazianzen[3] relates that in his day Christians celebrated their wedding anniversaries every year. But we will hold a fitting celebration today of a particularly rare and holy marriage, one which is an example of exquisite virtue. In this way we will give praise to God and our true respect to true virtue, and we will show our Venerable Grand Master our love, devotion, and gratitude . . .'

"When he finished, the Venerable Deputy Master turned to

the Grand Master through the organ to ask him to accept the congratulations and heartfelt good wishes of all the brethren of this our esteemed fraternal lodge on his silver anniversary of marriage to his most esteemed spouse . . . Then the Venerable Deputy Master suggested to the brethren that when we accept someone into our Masonic order [sign of circle] we give him women's gloves so that he might give them to the woman he chooses as his lawful Freemasoness, as an expression from our Masonic order's [circle] sincere respect for the female sex, though for certain fundamental reasons we cannot enroll women into its society. And if our Masonic order [circle] presents such a gift to a woman we do not even know, entrusting the newly appointed brother to make a worthy choice, then it is all the more fitting for our Sacred Masonic order [circle] to give its sincere respect to our sister whom we do know and esteem, our sister and the spouse and loyal helpmate of our Venerable Grand Master, who, as all our brethren know, is a true, active Freemasoness in her fraternal virtue and sincere love for us. We want to show her our completely brotherly, heartfelt love and sincere gratitude for all this. And as proof of our deep, inner indebtedness to her, what sort of outward gift might we bring this sister whom we esteem so highly? As an outward expression, the gloves, though they be meager, are quite important according to the hieroglyphs and our subject. And this present from all of us in our honorable lodge [square] to our long-time esteemed sister . . . conveys to her in all her humility proof of the unspoken love that all our brethren feel toward her, as well as being a new symbol of our fraternal union's gratitude and complete devotion to her most precious spouse . . . They further agreed that the Venerable Deputy Master would convey this unanimous position for us, and he ordered the first and second wardens to go to our most esteemed sister tomorrow at midday, and between them to bring her the women's gloves on a blue pillow . . ."

The lodge's resolution was put into effect. The Masonic gloves were brought to A. E. Labzina. In the lodge's protocols, assembled meticulously by month, it was noted: "The previous protocol included the Deputy Master's proposal regarding

bearing gloves in the name of the entire lodge [square] of
D[ying] S[phinx] to our most esteemed sister and the spouse
of our Venerable Grand Master, as a sign of special respect for
her. Since then the h[onorable] brother, the second warden,
has reported that, in carrying out this order given to him, the
esteemed sister Anna Evdokimovna accepted the symbolic gift
of the lodge [square] with heartfelt gratitude and fell to her
knees with the deepest reverence. The Venerable Grand Master
added to this that the esteemed sister had requested that he
place these gloves on her coffin when she died."

Notes

THE MEMOIR

1. Labzina's father, Evdokim Yakovlevich Yakovlev, died in 1764 at the age of 71. Thus, he was 66 when Labzina was born. Her mother was 40 years his junior (born 1732, died 1772). Labzina composed an alternative introduction to her memoir, one that gave much more attention to her father as her source of spiritual guidance (see appendix 1 for the text).

2. St. Petersburg was the new capital of the Russian Empire, founded at the beginning of the eighteenth century by Emperor Peter the Great (1672–1725). The Yakovlevs were provincial gentry and lived about one thousand miles away from the capital near the Ural mining town of Ekaterinburg.

3. The Eucharist is a particularly holy sacrament in Christianity, western and eastern, signifying communion with the body and blood of Christ.

4. Here and throughout the memoir Labzina uses the word "unfortunate" to refer to convicts, i.e., people whose fortunes have fallen and whose souls need ministration. For the sake of intelligibility we will call them convicts, except where the more emotional term seems particularly relevant.

5. It had become commonplace for members of the nobility to learn to read and write, although less so for women than for men. At this time Russia had very few schools for reading and writing. Thus, almost all literacy instruction took place either at home or with a private tutor. Labzina almost certainly learned to read before learning to write, and the ladder of instruction available to her was based on religious and Biblical texts: ABC books, books of hourly prayers, and the Gospels.

6. The references to black bread and the lack of tea are meant to show the simplicity of Labzina's diet. By this time, the well-to-do nobility preferred white bread—made of highly refined flour—over the coarser but more nutritious black bread. Tea had entered Russia via China in the late sixteenth or early seventeenth century and was considered a luxury until well into the nineteenth century.

7. Cabbage soup *(shchi)* and kasha, which could mean any type of cooked grain but usually referred to buckwheat groats, were considered peasant fare.

8. A verst is equivalent to about two-thirds of a mile.

9. The region where Labzina was living was home to several prisons and penal colonies, owing to its remoteness from major population centers and its proximity to the mines, where convicts often were sent to work.

10. Here and elsewhere in the text Labzina employs this type of impersonal phraseology, "there was a man at our house," to convey social distance. In this case the man was almost certainly a household servant, and very likely a serf.

11. Andrei Abramovich Irman was a career officer in the army, who had been given a series of commands over the industrial and mining regions of the southern and middle Urals.

12. Labzina's childhood home in the countryside outside of Ekaterinburg was itself considered a remote assignment. Barnaul was even farther away, on the unsettled frontier near Central Asia fully eight hundred miles southeast of Ekaterinburg.

13. Although unusual, it was not unknown for noblewomen to be responsible for estate management, especially when they were widowed, like Labzina's mother. Noblewomen could inherit land, and recent research has shown that they bought and sold land far more often than had been suspected.

14. See the alternative account of her father's death in appendix 1.

15. Here we see the common association made at the time between honest "women's work" and sewing or handicrafts. One need not speculate very hard to imagine what the dishonorable forms of wage labor would have been.

16. Tatars are a Turkic people, direct descendents of the Tatar invaders who conquered most of Rus in the early thirteenth century. Although their political control ended by the sixteenth century, large Tatar settlements remained, mostly on the eastern shore of the lower Volga River and in the Crimean Peninsula. This passage reflects the fact that Tatar and Russian populations did intermingle in the area around Ekaterinburg, but in the eyes of most Russians, Tatars were associated with danger, brigandage, and violence.

17. Bashkirs were another Turkic people in the region. Organized into large tribal units, they too were seen as wild and threatening, hence the image of a marauding band. During the seventeenth and eighteenth centuries the Bashkirs participated in some of the

largest and most threatening revolts in the Russian Empire, such as the Pugachev revolt (1771–1774), often joining with other non-Russian groups, Cossacks, and even Russian peasants in mass revolts, many of which originated in this region.

18. The term "orphan" *(sirota)* had a broad meaning in Labzina's day. Here it refers to fatherless children, even though they still have a mother. The term could also refer to people who see themselves as dependent on others, usually from a higher social rank, for protection and care. This usage of "orphan" can be found in many texts and supplications dating back centuries, predicated on the idea of collective honor, in which everyone ultimately falls under the protection of someone more powerful.

19. "Bread and salt" is a traditional Russian phrase and peasant custom, meaning hospitality. When strangers approached a village, a group of villagers would meet them at the edge of the community with a gift of bread and salt as a way of extending them welcome.

20. The steward or bailiff *(burmistr)* was an estate manager, typically a peasant, who served as the landlord's representative in the fields and in the peasant community. It was his responsibility to make certain that order was kept, that the fields were worked, and that the wishes of the landlord were carried out.

21. Atamans were chieftans, or heads of Cossack tribal groups. There were several Cossack hosts settled in the southern Urals at this time, and they tended to be among the more rebellious populations in the Russian Empire. Rogue or outlaw atamans were not uncommon, in large part because of growing resentment against what they saw as encroachments by the central government against their traditional autonomy.

22. The Demidov family owned one of the largest complexes of mines and metallurgical factories in all of Russia, dating back to the seventeenth century.

23. Calling people by their patronymic ("Kostentinovna") is a common form of expressing familiarity in Russian. Labzina gives the name an odd spelling here, as normally the name would be "Konstantinovna." One doesn't know whether the misspelling is deliberate, but it should be noted that Labzina's spelling and grammar were far from perfect, a possible reflection of her relative lack of formal schooling.

24. Aleksandr Matveevich Karamyshev, the author's future husband (see introduction). The formal and polite way to refer to an adult in Russian is by the first name and patronymic, which derives

from the father's first name. Thus Aleksandr Karamyshev's father was named Matvei, and in most polite company he would be called Aleksandr Matve*evich*. Similarly the author is Anna Evdokimovna Labzina (née Yakovleva), by which it is clear that her father was Evdokim Yakovlev.

25. Labzina was just thirteen at the time. This was young for a Russian noblewoman to be engaged, but not extraordinarily so, especially if her economic well-being or inheritance depended upon it.

26. The week before Easter. The usual adjective is *Strastnaia* (passionate), but Labzina uses *Strashnaia* (terrible), possibly prefiguring the trials that await her.

27. In all probability Labzina is referring to the Gospels here. It should be noted that the Bible did not circulate nearly as broadly in Russian society as it did in the rest of Europe, particularly Protestant Europe. Moreover, at the time in question the only printed Bibles were in Church Slavonic rather than modern Russian. The ability to read the Bible at her age demonstrates that she had progressed rather far up the ladder of literacy texts, and that she had been taught her ABCs in the traditional manner.

28. Beyond politeness, the request to be "accepted as a son" reflected the importance of dowries in prenuptial negotiations. The dowry and whatever land the bride might inherit from her parents constituted her own possessions, but typically the groom's family, in whose house the newlyweds usually lived, wanted the dowry to be placed under the control of the groom. Thus, to be accepted "as a son" meant to be trusted with a portion of the bride's family's material goods and land just as a son would be.

29. Had Labzina's mother died before the betrothal, Labzina would have been an underaged orphan, whose rights to family property and dowry would have been problematic. She thus could have found herself with no land, no means of support, and no network of protectors or benefactors. It was this extreme vulnerability that moved Labzina's mother to arrange the hasty marriage to Karamyshev.

30. The reference here is to princes or princelings, of which Russia was replete, thanks to the survival of numerous princely clans from medieval times.

31. Vera Alekseevna Karamysheva was his niece. Throughout the text, Labzina abbreviates her name to "Vera Alek." or simply "V. A." For simplicity's sake we have chosen to spell her name out in full in most places.

32. Vespers are the evening service.

33. Russian currency had become standardized in the eighteenth century, based on the ruble and kopeck. As today, there were one hundred kopecks to the ruble. Older coins, including the *grivna, den'ga,* and *al'tyn,* each of which was worth a fraction of a kopeck, were at this time being phased out of circulation. It is difficult to speak with any precision about the value, or purchasing power, of the eighteenth-century ruble. The century witnessed a major price inflation in Russia, and a rapid expansion of the money supply. As one point of comparison, three hundred rubles would have been equivalent to the annual salary of a midrange army officer.

34. These peasants were probably the serfs living on the Yakovlev estate.

35. The particular rites referred to here *(pominovenie)* entailed reading the names of the living and the dead members of the family in the liturgy as a form of remembrance for forty days after a death.

36. A reference both to St. Petersburg and to the life of high society that it implies.

37. I.e., tuberculosis.

38. See note 20.

39. Notice the intricate lines of authority here. Karamyshev was the head of his own family, and thus beyond his mother's control, but his wife was a member of the larger household headed by Karamyshev's mother, who was in a position to overrule Karamyshev in determining where Labzina would live.

40. Olonets is a region north of St. Petersburg and on the border of Finland. In the eighteenth century it was a center of metallurgy, specifically iron smelting.

41. The Solovetskii Islands, far north off the shore of the White Sea, were home to a renowned monastery, founded in the fourteenth century. It was the site of a protracted revolt by local monks and peasants as part of the Old Believer schism from the official church in the late seventeenth century. Miracles were supposed to have occurred there, first when the monastery was founded, and then in the late seventeenth century when the official church regained physical control of the site.

42. Much of northern and eastern Russia was covered by tundra, a form of permafrost in which root systems remain too shallow to support tree growth.

43. Age was closely connected to status in Russian society, and the term "elder" implied someone who held a position of authority

among his peers. Since physical laborers were commonly organized into work teams (artels), the elder would normally be a senior, experienced worker who had direct responsibility for the entire work group.

44. Petrozavodsk was slightly south of Olonets, and it too was a center of metallurgical factories, as well as being an iron-mining area.

45. Located in the far north of European Russia, Petrozavodsk experiences extremes of sunlight and darkness, as Labzina describes. In early summer it has white nights, in which the sun stays out almost perpetually. Conversely, early winter sees almost perpetual darkness.

46. The Russian term *zemlianka* means literally "earthen hut." Domiciles were made of densely packed mud, a cheap and quick mode of construction, but one that is unduly damp.

47. Lapland was an area of Finland next to Petrozavodsk inhabited mostly by seminomadic tribes (the Lapps) that followed the vast reindeer herds. Labzina accurately conveys the sparseness of population in that region.

48. Probably a reference to Andrei Fedorovich Deriabin, a career mining officer who later served as the director of the Mining and Salt Mine Department of the Russian Empire.

49. M. M. Kheraskov (1733–1807) was one of the leading figures of Russian intellectual life in his day. A product of an elite education in the Infantry Corps of Cadets, he spent the 1760s in Moscow serving in various administrative capacities at the newly opened (1755) Moscow University. Between 1770 and 1778 he served, as Labzina notes, as vice president of the College of Mines, and then he returned to Moscow University. During this time he was a central presence in Russian letters, a leading Freemason and poet, who came to be called "Russia's Homer" because of his epic poetry of the Russian past, particularly "Rossiada." "Rossiada" was intended as a truly national epic, focusing on the taking of Kazan in 1551 by Tsar Ivan IV (the Terrible), an accomplishment that brought to an end the last vestige of the Tatar yoke and symbolized Muscovy's emergence as a fully independent power. "Rossiada" also brought considerable favor to Kheraskov because its theme of Russian conquest appealed to the empress. Both in Petersburg and Moscow, then, Kheraskov's home became the site of numerous literary events and social gatherings among the political and intellectual elite.

50. In 1721 Peter the Great had reorganized Russian administration into a series of twelve colleges, one of which was the College

of Mines. Peter chose this model over the more common ministerial one because he wanted the agencies to be run by administrative cohorts, a mix of Russian officers and foreign specialists, rather than by individual ministers.

51. The use of the first name and patronymic denoted a tone of formality, in this case reflecting both the respectful tone that a junior officer would use in relation to a superior, and a somewhat subtler expression of emotional distance between Labzina and her husband. Indeed, nowhere in the text does Anna Evdokimovna use affectionate or diminutive terms for her husband, one of many stylistic techniques she employs to manipulate the reader's sympathies.

52. "Honest Criminal, or A Child's Love for His Parents," was a play by the French comic playwright Charles Georges Fenouillot de Falbaire de Quigney (1727–1800). I. A. Dmitrevskii, who also was an actor, translated the play into Russian in 1771.

53. This is a reference to the Treaty of Kuchuk Kainarji of July 1774 which ended the Russo-Turkish War of 1768–1774, the most recent in a series of conflicts between the two empires. Labzina has gotten the times a bit confused here, since the events being described took place in 1775.

54. Kheraskova (1737–1809), the wife of M. M. Kheraskov, Labzina's benefactor. Kheraskova was an intellectual in her own right, a poetess and translator, as well as the organizer of the literary salons in their house.

55. Prince Grigorii Aleksandrovich Potemkin-Tavricheskii, a general and one of the most prominent figures of the era, was the favorite of the empress for several years during the 1770s. Long after their romantic connection had ended, Potemkin remained the empress's friend and advisor, accompanying her on her famous southern tour in 1787, from which the myth of Potemkin villages derives. Potemkin was, thus, a man of enormous influence (and wealth), and to be a member of his entourage was highly desirable for an ambitious young nobleman. Potemkin was also renowned for his charm and love for the wild life, a reputation that Kheraskov confirms in this passage. On the other hand, Labzina depicts him as mostly a kindly and helpful ally in her efforts to rein in her husband's vices, and she appeals to "the Prince" a number of times over the head of Karamyshev's immediate superior, Nartov (see note 57).

56. Tsarskoe Selo was a suburban town outside of the capital where Catherine the Great had built a palace and to which she frequently retired. During her reign an entire community grew up

around her there, consisting largely of well-heeled noble families wishing to travel with the court and remain as part of the empress's retinue. Peterhof, or Petrodvorets, was another suburban palace, built largely during the reign of Peter the Great, and a short boat ride up the Neva River from St.Petersburg. Peterhof is famous for its Italianate splendor and fountains, and it served as a site of formal imperial celebrations, parades, and processions during the eighteenth and nineteenth centuries.

57. Andrei Andreevich Nartov (1737–1813) was Karamyshev's immediate superior at this time. A prominent writer and translator, he served under Potemkin in a variety of capacities. Between 1772 and 1779 he worked in the Mining College in a special department on minting coinage.

58. I.e., the Infantry Corps of Cadets.

59. By "bondsman" *(rab)* Labzina probably means a household serf.

60. By this "more senior supervisor" he may have meant Prince Potemkin (see note 55), or Mikhail Fedorovich Soimonov, president of the College of Mines (see below). According to Labzina, both men were helpful to her as she struggled to overcome Nartov's influence on her husband.

61. Bathhouses have long enjoyed great popularity in Russia as respectable places for cleansing and socializing. Bathhouses could be segregated by sex, but mixed baths were far from uncommon in the eighteenth century. In this instance, however, the bath in question was most disreputable, or so thought Labzina.

62. Catherine the Great, who reigned from 1762 to 1796.

63. A tax farmer *(otkupshchik)* was a franchisee, usually a local official, given responsibility for collecting taxes in exchange for a portion of the receipts. Because of the chronic paucity of available civil servitors, the Russian government continued to rely upon contractual or informal relationships such as these to administer the countryside well into the nineteenth century.

64. "The bestial sort of love" refers, presumably, to adultery, but the langauge is ambiguous and could mean sex without love, or, in light of the virginal manner in which Labzina constructs herself, even sex in general.

65. See note 52 above.

66. To be inscribed in a regiment was highly prestigious for a young officer, especially when the award came from an illustrious person such as Potemkin. The most prestigious regiments were in the cavalry, especially the guards' regiments. However,

the infantry regiment still constituted a desirable post.

67. Poltava is a town in southern Russia (in contemporary Ukraine) north of the Black Sea. Throughout the eighteenth century it was a military stronghold and a site of regimental importance, owing to its relative proximity to the Ottoman Empire and the Crimea.

68. This soliloquy is remarkable for its sordid picture of the court and its celebration of the family as the true basis of moral support. Astonishingly, Labzina is being warned against the most prominent figures in the empire, who come across as purveyors of vice and depravity, falsehood and flattery.

69. Probably Princess Elena Nikitichna Viazemskaia (1745–1832), sister of the Trubetskoi brothers, who were notable Freemasons.

70. St. Petersburg is made up largely of islands, through which run a series of canals and rivers. Kamennyi ostrov (Rock Island) is one of the smaller of these islands.

71. St. Peter was more or less the patron saint of the new capital, St. Petersburg, and thus it made sense to celebrate his name day at Peterhof (Peter's House or possibly Peter's Court). All of these "Peters," of course harkened back to Peter the Great (1672–1725), the founder of the empire, and thus the name day amounted to a celebration of the empire itself.

72. This is another case in which Labzina changes her spelling of a name.

73. *Pan* is the respectful way to address a Polish man, rather like "Sir" or "Mr.," and Labzina uses it to show that Golynski is Polish. She also suggests a number of Polonisms in his speech, both in pronunciation and terminology. He calls her *Pani,* for example, which is the female counterpart of Pan, and says *dobrze,* which is a common Polish phrase meaning "good" or "OK."

74. He was named to this position in May 1779. Russia had a small number of banks at this time, mostly state banks that received interest on loans, noble land banks, which allowed the nobility to take out mortgages, and a few paper currency and merchants' banks that facilitated foreign trade and extended short-term credit. It is not clear to which of these institutions Labzina is referring here, but Potemkin was actively involved in the project to create a central state bank. This may have been a local office in distant Irkutsk in south-central Siberia north of Mongolia, useful in Russia's Far Eastern trade.

75. Yaroslavl is a city on the upper Volga River, about one hundred miles northeast of Moscow. It was an important administrative

and trade center during the eighteenth century, thanks to its central location and access to waterways, which made it a fixture on the canal system that connected Russia's rivers.

76. Major General Franz Klichka was governor of Irkutsk from 1778–1783. The vice governor was Alexander von Zadelman.

77. Labzina uses an ambiguous word here, *devka,* which may mean simply a young unmarried woman, or depending upon the context, a servant girl, or even a "wench." In the memoir, "devka" is used when a young woman has involved herself in morally loose behavior. Thus, Vera Alexandrovna, whose name Labzina could barely bring herself to write, is referred to throughout as "devka."

78. Bleeding, or bloodletting, was a well-known treatment for a variety of maladies in the eighteenth century. It was thought that blood contained ill humors and could get too hot, thus requiring that the patient have some blood drained, typically from the arm. Bloodletting was a treatment of choice for female "hysteria."

79. Nerchinsk is located on the Amur River, just north of the Chinese border, in the Russian Far East.

80. When convicts were sent to hard labor in Siberia, they often lived in villages amidst the local population. Many times they were branded or had their nostrils slit as a way of marking them, so that everyone would know that they were convicts.

81. Labzina endowed the encounters with Feklist with great importance. They are the only pieces of the memoir that she published in her lifetime, in an article published in 1817 in the Masonic journal, *The Messenger of Zion,* which was edited by her second husband, Aleksandr Labzin.

82. Nikolai Irinarkhovich Ozerov, who remained in exile and died there in 1790. He was the uncle of the noted writer, V. A. Ozerov. We were unable to find biographical information on Zhilin.

83. As previous editors have noted, Labzina's timeline gets very confused here. They stayed in Nerchinsk for one and a half years. Thus the tearful departure described above was from Nerchinsk back to Irkutsk some time in mid–1781.

84. Labzina uses an unusual word here, *roditel'nitsa,* which literally means "the woman who gave birth to me." She may do this to distinguish her birth mother from her mother-in-law, whom she now calls mother.

85. Apparently there was an entail on Karamyshev's property, so that his wife would retain possession of it only if they had children. Since they had none, she faced losing everything when he died. In

her eyes he is presenting her with an utterly immoral proposition, but it is possible to see it as a creative (if not strictly aboveboard) way of assuring her material well-being after his death.

86. Johann Arndt (1555–1621), one of the most important mystical and pietistic thinkers of his day. Arndt's work was much admired and read—usually in translation—by the more mystical of Russia's Freemasons. It is rather surprising that Labzina was already reading this type of mystical philosophy while still married to Karamyshev, who clearly had no interest in it. It may be an indication of Kheraskov's influence.

87. A household *bania* is a small outbuilding resembling a Finnish sauna. In contrast to the disreputable bathhouse discussed earlier in the memoir, this one would have been entirely respectable.

THE DIARY

1. Iurii Nikitich Bartenev, a member of the Dying Sphinx Masonic Lodge (inducted in October 1817) and a passionate devotee of Labzina's husband, Aleksandr Fedorovich Labzin. The future husband of Labzina's ward, her niece Ekaterina Stepanovna Mikulina, both of whose parents had died when she was a small child.

2. Aleksandra Petrovna Khvostova (1758–1828), the niece of the noted writer M. M. Kheraskov, wife of a prominent member of Dying Sphinx. Khvostova was herself an active participant in the activities of Dying Sphinx, and as the diary makes clear, something of a rival to Labzina, who blames her for many of the misfortunes befalling her husband.

3. Vera Aleksandrovna Leonrod (1793–1872), raised by Khvostova, would marry another leading member of Dying Sphinx, F. I. Prianishnikov in November 1818.

4. Jackstraws is a game played with strips of straw or wood.

5. Here Labzina is referring to a growing split within Dying Sphinx that contributes to the decline of its standing in the eyes of the government and its ultimately being banned in 1822, resulting at least indirectly in Labzin's exile. The government was growing increasingly wary that secret societies were dens of sedition and conspiracy, hence the general ban. Labzin's personal exile came as a result of insulting remarks he made about several imperial protégés, but must be seen against the backdrop of a growing suspicion of Freemasonry, as well as Labzin's own cantankerous personality. The latter seeps through Labzina's diary in her

accounts of the "disloyalty" of so many of his followers.

6. Gehenna is literally a valley near Jerusalem, but within the Judeo-Christian tradition Gehenna is typically used metaphorically to refer to the place of future torment, or hell.

7. I.e., Dying Sphinx

8. Part of the shock and demoralization to which Labzina refers comes from the intense assault on Labzin by his various critics among the intellectual and political upper crust of St. Petersburg. The onslaught so dejected him that he decided to cease publication of *Messenger of Zion*.

9. An *arshin* is a measure of length equivalent to 2.33 feet.

10. Anna Fedorovna Labzina, Labzin's sister and Anna Evdokimovna's sister-in-law.

11. Here and elsewhere in the text Labzina invokes these apocalyptic images of the Second Coming to cope with her own grief and misgivings.

12. Among all the Freemasonic lodges of the time, Dying Sphinx was renowned as philosophically the most serious, the most mystical, and the most committed to Christian doctrine. Other lodges, by contrast, had the reputation of being far looser, little more than social clubs for whom the elaborate and secret rituals of membership served mainly for fraternal bonding. Labzina, then, is lamenting what she perceives to be the deterioration of Dying Sphinx into just one among many Masonic social clubs.

13. Probably a reference to Prianishnikov.

14. Aleksandr Petrovich Martynov, a prominent member of the lodge who was named junior warden in 1818.

15. Katia is Labzina's niece, Ekaterina Mikulina.

16. Her fiancé was Bartenev (see note 1).

17. Sof'ia Alekseevna Mudrova, whom, like Ekaterina, Labzina considered to be her ward. Mudrova was the niece of a prominent professor at Moscow University, Matvei Iakovlevich Mudrov, and her father had been a part of Labzin's circle. Orphaned at a young age, she was raised by the Labzins, to whom she remained very devoted and whose legacy she celebrated in her own memoirs: "Vospominaniia Sof'i Alekseevny Laikevich," *Russkaia starina* (1905), no. 4, especially 171–88.

18. Labzina's use of "republic" and "brotherhood" bears some mention here. She seems to be suggesting that brotherhoods constitute unions of equals built upon family bonds of loyalty, love, and respect. Republics, by contrast, seem to be assemblages of equals with

no affective bonds, a chaotic mass of selfish individuals.

19. The Mother of God typically was called upon in Russian Orthodoxy to intercede with God or Jesus to help ease one's sufferings. This image of maternal intercession appears to have been important to Labzina's religious outlook, as versions of it recur in her memoir as well.

20. It is interesting to compare Labzina's version of this soap opera with Bartenev's. On the very day when Labzina wrote this entry Bartenev wrote the following letter to his brother:

My Dear Brother and Friend Vsevolod Nikitich,

As a testament of my regard and love for you I hasten to thank you again for all the favors, for all the affection that you have always and everywhere shown me. Can it be that you would refuse even now to oblige me [with] your brotherly love? . . . For the past two years, specifically since December 9, 1816, I have been visiting a certain young woman, the daughter of Major General Mikulin, who served in the Corps of Engineers. From that very time my heart began to favor her as a friend. Ever since then I have tried to get to know her and have found that Providence is showing me in this kind maiden that which I have diligently sought out in others. I spoke to you about her already [when we were] in the countryside. She is an orphan, without means, but rich in her heart, rich in humility and Christian precepts. In a word, I am firmly resolved to belong to no one but her, and I have assured her of this with the word of honor of an honest man and Christian. She has accepted my proposal, and her relative, her natural uncle, Alexander Fedorovich Labzin, to whom I am obliged for my being reborn, has given his consent. What is lacking is the main piece, specifically the blessing of her progenitress, without whom even the Lord God will not sanctify and cannot consecrate our union. The time for consummating our joy remains unresolved, for without her mother's approval I am unable to make any plans. I ask you, dear brother, to act in this most august matter on my behalf. Your intercession can be very useful to me. My illness, thank God it has passed, has cost me a lot! My doctor advises me that, in order to preserve my health, I should get married as soon as possible, and in that way preserve myself from succumbing to that which I, as you and I can testify, was always a victim. As he says, this will give some stability to my otherwise volatile character and will calm the hot-bloodedness of my temperament through the blessed influence of Christian matrimony. I appeal to you, or more precisely to your brotherly friendship and love, to work on this matter on my behalf. My future wife and I will be indebted to you for our happiness, and you, being like a father to me in receiving me from the baptismal font, will become both a father and blesser of our holy matrimony. This is how matters stand, dear brother. I will await your answer with great eagerness. They have been kind enough to [promise to] inform me as soon as the mail arrives, for a minute now seems like a hundred years . . . ("Pis'mo Iu. N. Barteneva bratu Vsevolodu Nikitichu, 25 oktiabria 1818 goda," *Sbornik starinnykh bumag khraniashchikhsia v muzee P. I. Shchukina* [Moscow, 1901], 8:422–23.)

21. This apparently refers to Prianishnikov's sister.

22. Vera Leonrod (see note 3).

23. The literal translation of the term Labzina employs here is "female prophet," an indication that she had specific women in mind. It is known that several of the brothers in Dying Sphinx, who were close to Tsar Alexander I, shared his fascination with seers, mystics, fortune tellers, etc. Seances were not unknown, and some even took alchemy seriously. This tendency seems to have influenced Labzin himself, and while the practices were too widespread within the milieu for Labzina to denounce them, it is clear that they make her very uneasy in their contradiction of religious precepts and their distortion of the doctrine of Mysteries of Faith.

24. A diminutive and affectionate form of Sofia or Sonia.

25. Yuliana Egorovna Sorokina, the wife of one of the lodge members.

26. This is a reference to a work, popular among Freemasons, *Das Heimweh,* written by the German author Johann Heinrich Jung (1740–1817), who wrote under the name of Heinrich Stilling. Jung Stilling, as he is usually called, was a leading German Pietist who tried, much like Dying Sphinx, to blend Enlightenment ideals of reason, rational statecraft, and individuality with a passionate Christian faith. Labzina seems to be suggesting that these passages were read aloud, and the soothing effect she describes is reminiscent of the way other religious writers responded to recitations from the Gospels or Psalms.

27. Labzina here is referring to two of Prianishnikov's friends,

Nikolai Stepanovich Kozhukhov and Vsevolod Nikandrovich Zhadovskoi. Like Prianishnikov, they both were members of Dying Sphinx, and both came from privileged noble families.

28. Artemii presumably was the servant who managed the Labzin household. This entire lament about finances and household management provides a useful window into the economics of noble life, the costs involved, and the organization of domesticity. Servants, coachmen, stewards, and the like were a necessary fact of life in the Labzin home in the capital, and they had to be paid and cared for. All of this was expensive, especially if one lacked a high-paying position in state service and a remunerative estate. Labzin evidently was too involved with his religious and literary pursuits to devote any attention to household expenses. Without Artemii the household seemed not to function, and in his absence, it was left to Labzina, who had no income of her own, to worry about the mundane business of paying the bills.

29. Bartenev.

30. Alexandra Ivanovna Kozhukhova, wife of Nikolai Stepanovich Kozhukhov.

31. Apparently one of Labzina's household serfs.

32. B. L. Modzalevskii believes that this was a reference to P. I. Albychev, a lodge member who was expelled in 1820 along with several others as part of the split in Dying Sphinx to which Labzina continually alludes.

33. From the context it is clear that Zakhar was a household serf for whom Labzina felt a degree of manorial responsibility. An episode like this says a great deal about status in early-nineteenth-century Russia. Recall that Labzina never considered police intervention in her first marriage or in the brawling that took place at her home then. Those were family matters, and it was considered unseemly to take such drastic action as to summon the authorities for a domestic issue within a noble family. Zakhar was a peasant, however, and Labzina never thought twice about calling in the police to subdue him.

APPENDIX 2

1. This text is excerpted from: Tira Sokolovskaia, "Podnesenie masonskikh perchatok A. E. Labzinoi. Epizod iz istorii russkogo masonstva (1819)," *Russkii arkhiv* (1905), no. 12: 532–35.

2. The translations for Masonic terminology are taken from

Douglas Smith, *Working the Rough Stone: Freemasonry and Society in Eighteenth-Century Russia* (DeKalb, Ill.: Northern Illinois University Press, 1998).

    3. St. Gregory Nazianzen "the Theologian" (c. 329–395), Bishop of Constantinople, Doctor of the Church, Son of St. Nonna and St. Gregory the Elder, Bishop of Nazianzus. St. Gregory sought a solitary life, but his father forced him into the priesthood, and later St. Basil made him bishop of Sasima against his wishes. His health drove him into seclusion in 375, but he emerged to lead the church in Constantinople, where faith had been eroding. He is celebrated for his sermons on the Trinity and for his religious poetry. *Butler's Lives of the Saints,* ed. H. Thurston and D. Attwater (New York, 1956), 2:255–59.

Index

7/17/2015